"Perspectives, lifelines, and insights are richly revealed in this sensitively told story of youth in juvenile justice systems who have struggled to make meaning out of loss and adversity. This is a worthwhile read for anyone who cares about troubled teens, including parents, teachers, and those who work in the juvenile justice field."

> —Patricia Chamberlain, Ph.D., founder of Multidimensional Treatment Foster Care

"This book vividly describes—in their own words—the gripping stories of troubled kids who grew up in dysfunctional families and often were not helped by disjointed systems. But it tells another story: how good programs and good people helped them turn their lives around. As a bonus, the juvenile justice system authors tell readers what works—and doesn't work—and why. All readers will be rewarded for going along on the journey."

> —James C. Howell, Ph.D., criminologist

"The field of juvenile justice is not for the fainthearted. It can be exciting and challenging, but also incredibly rewarding. Not only have Lisa, John, and Linda provided the background stories to help us better understand why this work is so important, but they also have laid out a road map for improving the system. By following the four basic principles of 'who,' 'what,' 'how,' and 'how well,' the juvenile justice system can become more effective and humane. Just as important, they have helped expose the ineffective practices that are so often used in the juvenile justice system. We are unlikely to change much behavior through talk therapy, education-based interventions, scaring them straight, or get-tough approaches. I applaud the work of Lisa, John, and Linda, and I hope that others find this book as thought-provoking and insightful as I did."

> —Edward J. Latessa, Ph.D., Center for Criminal Justice Research

ABOUT THE AUTHORS

JOHN AARONS is a casework coordinator with the Lane County Department of Youth Services in Oregon. Previously he worked as a consultant for the National Council for Juvenile and Family Court Judges and his articles have been published in a number of sociology, psychology, and science journals.

LISA SMITH is the director of the Lane County Department of Youth Services. She has worked in and with the juvenile justice system for many years.

LINDA WAGNER has worked as the research and development coordinator in the Lane County Department of Youth Services for twenty years, tracking juvenile crime, measuring juvenile re-offense rates, and evaluating the impact of juvenile justice policy and system reform.

All are frequent speakers on the subject of juvenile crime. They live in Oregon.

Dispatches
from
Juvenile Hall
Fixing a Failing System

John Aarons, Lisa Smith, and Linda Wagner

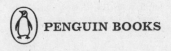
PENGUIN BOOKS

PENGUIN BOOKS
Published by the Penguin Group
Penguin Group (USA) Inc., 375 Hudson Street, New York, New York 10014, U.S.A.
Penguin Group (Canada), 90 Eglinton Avenue East, Suite 700, Toronto, Ontario,
Canada M4P 2Y3 (a division of Pearson Penguin Canada Inc.)
Penguin Books Ltd, 80 Strand, London WC2R 0RL, England
Penguin Ireland, 25 St Stephen's Green, Dublin 2, Ireland (a division of Penguin Books Ltd)
Penguin Group (Australia), 250 Camberwell Road, Camberwell, Victoria 3124, Australia
(a division of Pearson Australia Group Pty Ltd)
Penguin Books India Pvt Ltd, 11 Community Centre, Panchsheel Park,
New Delhi - 110 017, India
Penguin Group (NZ), 67 Apollo Drive, Rosedale, North Shore 0632,
New Zealand (a division of Pearson New Zealand Ltd)
Penguin Books (South Africa) (Pty) Ltd, 24 Sturdee Avenue, Rosebank,
Johannesburg 2196, South Africa

Penguin Books Ltd, Registered Offices:
80 Strand, London WC2R 0RL, England

First published in Penguin Books 2009

10 9 8 7 6 5 4 3 2 1

Copyright © John Aarons, Lisa Smith, and Linda Wagner, 2009
All rights reserved

LIBRARY OF CONGRESS CATALOGING IN PUBLICATION DATA
Aarons, John, date.
  Dispatches from juvenile hall : fixing a failing system / John Aarons, Lisa Smith, and Linda
Wagner.
    p. cm. — (Penguin books)
  Includes bibliographical references.
  ISBN 978-0-14-311622-6
  1. Juvenile justice, Administration of—United States. 2. Juvenile delinquents—United
States. I. Smith, Lisa, date. II. Wagner, Linda, date. III. Title.
  HV9104.A612 2009
  364.360973—dc22
                        2009006221

Printed in the United States of America
Set in Janson Text
Designed by Sabrina Bowers

Disclaimer

Although the stories in this book are true, certain names, locations, and identifying characteristics have been changed to protect the privacy of some of the individuals portrayed.

This book is dedicated to the courageous people willing to make juvenile justice reform in order to reduce victimization, turn young lives around, and make our communities safer places.

Acknowledgments

Writing a book about fixing the juvenile justice system takes more than three, thirty, or even fifty people. It stands on the shoulders of decades of researchers and practitioners who have dedicated themselves to improving the lives of young people and their families across America. We are deeply indebted to Dr. Ed Latessa, who in addition to his leadership and stellar research generously gave us his counsel and guidance. The research of Dr. Don Andrews, Dr. Mark Lipsey, Dr. Mark Eddy, Dr. Jeff Sprague, and Dr. Patty Chamberlain has also been a catalyst for contemporary reform in the juvenile justice system. Their practical application of best practices research has transformed day-to-day probation work for those jurisdictions bold enough to stretch beyond the "just lock 'em up" slogans.

We are fortunate that in our work lives we are surrounded by talented professionals who teach us something each day about hard work, professionalism, and dedication. This book would have been impossible to complete without their presence in our lives. Special thanks to Christina McMahan, who served as our coordinator and muse; and to Robert L. Perry, Cheryl Schworm, Judge Ann Aiken, Stephen J. Carmichael, Wade Fraser, and Kenneth Viegas for leading by example on how to be change agents in a very inflexible system.

We would also like to thank our families for their inspiration, support, and sacrifices that they have made and continue to make so that we can realize our professional dreams to make a difference in the juvenile justice system. We couldn't have done this without the support of Pamela and Anna Aarons, Rian Anderson, Neva Bota, Mikaela Tuesday-Wagner, Greg, Jordan, and Taylor Smith, and Floy Ann and Don Hinrichsen.

Special thanks to our editor, Tom Roberge, for his guidance and support.

We want to especially thank the youths and professionals who so generously gave of their time and their personal experiences that really brought this book to life and gave it their voice.

Contents

Introduction

How often do you hear about proven ways to reduce juvenile crime? How often do you hear
about effective delinquency reduction programs
that are research-based rather than someone's personal opin-
ion about what "youths gone bad" really need? Juvenile crime
can have horrendous consequences, and while we hear more
and more about the gruesome crimes adolescents commit,
much less attention is placed on the proven and effective ways
to prevent or reduce juvenile crime. When those conversations
include effective ways to address delinquency, it quickly becomes apparent that there is more room for hope for these
youths than reasons to fear them.

The causes for concern are real, but often overestimated.
On any given morning, people turn on the TV, pick up a newspaper, or listen to the car radio during their commute and are
confronted with news items about teenagers committing
crimes that we can't imagine an adult doing. The images are
almost too ghastly to bear: teen boys forcing another boy to
rape his own mother and then beating both of them; the pro-

verbial quiet kid going to school and opening fire on his class-
mates and teachers; girls holding down a victim to cut off her
hair, beating her until she passes out, then writing the word
whore all over her body.

In the graphic telling of those horrific crimes committed
by adolescents, important information is lost. There is the fact
that such crimes, while gruesome and deserving of severe punishment, are rare. Think of it this way: If the population of the
United States comprised solely juvenile offenders, only those
living in Ohio would be considered violent. The rest of the nation's youth population would consist largely of juveniles whose
worst offense was to steal the latest superhero lunchbox from a
local store, and a small group who left their homes in the middle of the night because they couldn't bear to listen to their
drunken fathers beat their mothers again, and whose crime
was to break the windows of the parked cars they encountered—an act rooted in fear and anger. But people don't often
make such distinctions among the types of juvenile offenders,
and thereby treat these latter offenders much as they do the
more serious juvenile offenders, i.e., locking them up for long
periods of time. Yet research indicates that such incarceration
is not effective for the lower-risk juvenile, and can actually lead
him to commit more crimes when released from lockup. Sum-
marily throwing these types of juvenile offenders in prison can
have damaging unintended effects on generations of families.

The evolution of juvenile justice policies has not relied on
science or research regarding effective strategies for reducing
delinquency, but instead has been influenced by two strikingly
dissimilar and unrelated disciplines: adult corrections and child
welfare. While these disciplines provide effective services for
the populations they are designed to handle, they do not necessarily treat juvenile offenders in the most competent way,
one that reduces juvenile crime, or with the most cost-efficient

methods, at the lowest cost to the public. Research shows that when one is dealing with juvenile offenders, using the right intervention at the right time can lead to tremendous progress in preventing further criminal behavior. It also ensures that public funds are used to yield the most significant results possible for the investment made.

The blueprint for reducing juvenile crime is readily available to those who want to employ proven methods and bring about juvenile justice reform, who want to move away from the polarizing arguments of "soft on crime" versus "hard on crime," and, instead, implement strategies that are "smart on crime." Scientific studies based on robust research readily demonstrate which approaches work in reducing juvenile crime. These approaches offer real hope in the form of safer neighborhoods and more positively engaged adolescents. In addition, they are cost-effective, so that even the most financially strapped jurisdiction can afford to use them. Spending money on anything less than a proven approach is a misuse of public funds.

Unfortunately, proper understanding and dissemination of this instructional blueprint have been grossly limited. For too long, this is where juvenile justice administrators and elected officials have failed most egregiously, developing universal policies in response to the rare violent incident. The impact of violent crimes on victims' families, friends, and communities is devastating and requires an appropriate punitive response, but the measures customarily taken in response to violent crime by juveniles are not effective when dealing with the most common forms of juvenile delinquency. And yet there appears to be an unspoken agreement among policy makers that these punitive measures and the inherent "tough love" approach are to be used universally, without regard to a crime's severity or to any extenuating circumstances. In short, such an approach casts the juvenile justice system as a miniature version of the adult penal system, one that ignores the fact that the causes of juvenile crime, and thus the opportunities to deter it, are very different from those of adult criminal behavior. (It's also worth mentioning here that there has never been agreement that the adult system is successful.)

As expected, there is no shortage of emotionally charged opinions on the juvenile justice system or potential ways to fix it. The journey from adolescence to adulthood is often perilous, and those who traveled the path successfully years ago are not familiar with how the terrain has changed since their youthful odyssey. Adolescence is the single most significant time in human life where rapid physical and emotional changes occur. In tandem with this, adolescents begin testing their limits and pushing boundaries. Significant independence comes with numerous opportunities for danger at a time when a teenager feels infallible and immortal. The notion of installing metal detectors in schools was unfathomable in the 1970s and '80s, but they are now a common sight in many cities; schoolyard fights have evolved into full-blown assaults, with serious injuries and sometimes even deaths occurring. Also, children are now bombarded with information that just ten years ago would have been deemed wholly inappropriate. Violent images on television, in movie theaters, and on the Internet reinforce the notion that life is expendable, that death is easily mitigated with the mere push of the Reset button.

When out in public, juvenile justice workers are often in a state of perpetual fear; we dread being asked the most common conversation starter: "So what do you do for a living?" Honest responses are met with a wide variety of opinions on what to do with delinquent teens, but in our more than forty collective years of such informal discussions, we have never heard a single recommendation grounded in the research of what works.

It is obvious people have great passion for the topic, but passion without knowledge is like teen sex without a condom: there will be consequences. And the consequences when discussing juvenile justice are usually knee-jerk responses in favor of stern public policies aimed at *all* juvenile offenders, policies that should instead be reserved for the rare violent offender. Rather than solving or even addressing the problem, we, the communities with an abiding interest in helping these children, actually become a part of the problem. In fact, many of the most popular, and costly, programs have been shown to *increase* juvenile crime.

As a society, we are guilty of looking for easy answers to the extremely complex problems surrounding juvenile crime, but developing shortsighted responses only gives the appearance that we're doing something about the problem. Despite the daunting task, many opportunities exist to make real changes, to hold juvenile offenders accountable for their actions, and to increase public safety. When approaches are thoughtful and applied correctly, success in terms of rehabilitating juvenile offenders is not only possible but commonplace. No longer part of the problem, we then become leaders in turning the tide on juvenile crime. More important, in the course of reducing crime in our communities, we turn these young people around so that they can lead personally fulfilling lives and make positive contributions to the neighborhoods they once victimized.

Since there is no silver bullet, no one approach that fully addresses the complex juvenile delinquency problem, we must ask ourselves: What *does* work to reduce juvenile crime significantly and in the process turn young offenders' lives around?

Reducing juvenile crime is dependent on our addressing the problems that give rise to it. Hundreds of studies with juvenile offenders across the county have identified the risk factors that place teens at increased jeopardy of delinquency. Serious and chronic juvenile offenders have multiple risk factors in their lives and limited (or nonexistent) tools to deal with them. These risk factors include: acting out early in life (before the age of thirteen); experiencing negative peer association (i.e., hanging out with other adolescents who are getting in trouble); using alcohol and other drugs; struggling in school (e.g., repeatedly failing in the classroom); and facing extensive family problems. The last includes the pain and anxiety of having one or both parents involved in criminal activity (this is known as *family criminality*), substance abuse, and/or domestic violence in the home, and undergoing physical, emotional, and even sexual child abuse.

We all know, and perhaps even love, someone who had one or two of these risk factors during his childhood and yet didn't become a career criminal. If you were to ask that person how he made it through those difficult times, he would most likely recall a positive adult mentor or role model who held him accountable in a loving and fair manner, or a specific positive life experience, such as doing well in school, participating in sports or a club, or joining a spiritual community, all opportunities for adults and peers to model and encourage constructive behavior. These constitute protective factors.

Juvenile offenders who become criminals as adults have had many risk factors at the same time, and few protective factors to mitigate the problems associated with compounded risks. Since there is no one cause of juvenile criminality, there is no single approach capable of addressing all the risk factors, while at the same time holding the offenders accountable. The solution is a balance between punitive corrections responses and effective treatment that addresses the multiple risk factors in these children's and their families' lives. The two must work together.

Punitive responses hold offenders accountable for their actions and provide a degree of restoration to the community. They include restitution to victims, community service, electronic monitoring, short-term stays in local detention centers, and, in some cases, longer stays in state lockup facilities. However, punitive responses alone do not reduce juvenile delinquency, and many studies have shown that, on their own, these measures tend to increase the incidence of crime, a fact that challenges the popular "get tough on crime" agenda. That said, the "get smart on crime" agenda does not propose to do away with these practices. On the contrary, offenders must be held accountable and be subject to intensive supervision, and communities and victims must have restoration whenever possible. Furthermore, it's obvious that some juvenile offenders are too dangerous to be allowed to stay on the streets, and must be placed in secure lockup facilities. Without rehabilitative treatment, however, these children will most likely return to their communities without the skills they need to grow into more productive adults, people who won't continue to victimize others and who won't pass their criminal patterns on to their children, thereby continuing the cycle of family criminality.

To accomplish this, corrections responses must be balanced with rehabilitative treatment. Effective treatment must address the risk factors that place teens in increased jeopardy of delinquency. This includes drug treatment, education reinforcement, job readiness training, positive peer association, and personal skills building. Skills building works simultaneously to rectify criminal thinking and to teach behavior that represents an appropriate response to a high-stress situation, behavior that teens must master in real-life situations as part of their probation work. Examples of this include increasing refusal skills so the teens know how to respond to peers' attempts to engage them in criminal activities, or developing the skills necessary to identify and avoid high-risk situations, such as getting high at school. On the face of it, the logical response to behavior like this seems to be a matter of simple common sense: they are doing something horribly wrong and should just stop doing it, or be punished into stopping. But such an approach misses the mark. It's easy to see why that style doesn't work when we help teens make less serious behavioral changes. For example, when teaching a child to throw a baseball and seeing him continually throw it incorrectly, we don't think, "What's wrong with that kid?" Instead, we assume that he never learned the skill or, more accurately, that no one ever taught him the skill properly. He therefore must be taught correctly and must practice the new skill over and over again, until it comes naturally. The same applies to appropriate social behavior. For the most part, children model their behavior after adult role models, and with non-criminal family situations, it's never an issue. But with juvenile offenders, their criminal lives and the way they think about them seem normal to them; they are, after all, modeling their behavior on that of the negative models from their own lives. Thus, in order to teach them appropriate behavior, the same skills-building approach must be employed. Of course, they aren't kids on a baseball field, and there's much more at stake than a throwing error.

In addition, families must be part of the solution. Of course, in many cases the child's family is itself a risk factor, which means that treatment providers must be creative when identifying the significant adults in an offender's life. Sometimes both parents are raising the child; sometimes only one of them is, but a grandparent, aunt, or neighbor can also act as a surrogate parent. The point is that working with the juvenile alone ignores one of the greatest strengths in his or her life: family relationships. There are ways to engage families effectively and connect them to the support systems they need. The goal is not to have government agencies become or replace the parents, but, rather, to encourage the family to work with the child to develop the skills necessary to be successful.

In short, punitive responses show offenders that there are negative consequences for their actions, and rehabilitative treatments teach them new ways to react in risky situations. Unless these two approaches are used together and in a balanced manner, we are compromising public safety and wasting public funds. The good news is that when they are used together, and work to support each other in their efforts, recidivism (or re-offenses) decreases by about 50 percent for high-risk offenders.

Details on effective treatment programs, research into what works, the costs and benefits of approaching the issue correctly, and examples of specific programs, both successful and unsuccessful, are provided in this book. In addition, examples of how to engage high-risk families throughout the treatment process are described and supported with accounts from juveniles and families with experience in the juvenile justice system.

As this blueprint, or new road map, unfolds, it also includes an informal review of who is doing this really well, and asks why other community leaders are failing to promote proven approaches. Many jurisdictions have implemented best-practices programs, or at the very least have incorporated evidence-based practices into aspects of their programs. Unfortunately, vigorous implementation of evidence-based practices on a community-wide scale has not taken root in many jurisdictions.

In terms of leadership in efforts to reform the juvenile justice system, noted criminologists such as Dr. Edward Latessa of the University of Cincinnati have long championed a more scientific approach to developing crime prevention policies and intervention programs. Among our elected officials, it is much more common to hear criticisms of what doesn't work than to hear what we can do about changing these failing systems. Clearly this needs to change.

It is hoped, and there is great reason for hope, that this book will contribute to the national conversation about policies that actually succeed in preventing juvenile crime, practices that help to create long-lasting change among young offenders and their families, and alterations that the juvenile justice system can make in order to become a better steward of public funds. Through effective programming, public funding can be targeted with almost laser-like precision on the juveniles most in need of support and corrective influence. This would be a radical departure from the scattershot approach of distributing programming depending on the current political trend or a single horrific event. For community members passionate about, or even merely interested in, this important issue, the information in this book will provide them with tools that will enable them to move away from being part of the problem to lead the way with proven solutions.

In order to shed some light on the current state of affairs, this book includes an in-depth examination of a few so-called horrific offenses, surveying not just the perpetrators' criminal activity but also their entire life stories, alongside those of their victims. And we stress the importance of differentiating between these violent offenders and other juvenile delinquents. This book also outlines ways that communities can be smart on crime, and shows how more widespread personal interest in this can only benefit our communities—moving us away from being narrowly focused on the crimes themselves and returning us to being civic-minded.

This book listens to the voices of people in the system: juvenile offenders, their families, and people who work in and with the system. Included are offenders who will be locked up their entire lives, and offenders who have moved on from their criminal pasts and are now giving back to their communities, especially by helping others move away from their own criminal behavior and risk factors. We chose to transcribe directly the words of our interviewees, believing that nothing compares to the intimacy and immediacy of their actual voices. Providing the framework for each chapter, their stories are vivid examples of ways in which the juvenile justice system has been successful. By pointing to what works, these cases offer hope as we strive to reduce juvenile crime.

Part I

Personal Narratives

Chapter 1

Jasmine

Jasmine is a dark-haired, slender young woman of sixteen, although she appears to be in her mid-twenties and could easily be mistaken for a juvenile justice staff member instead of a probationer. Jasmine appeared friendly yet nervous when we met her for lunch at the local Applebee's restaurant to talk about her life and her experiences in the juvenile justice system. While we talked, she looked around the restaurant frequently and twisted her napkin around her fingers. She began in a matter-of-fact tone, that of a schoolgirl on a Monday morning telling her friends what happened over the weekend. But as we listened to her description of her early life, her tone belying the shocking nature of the details, we became increasingly uneasy; we were all parents, but nothing had prepared us for her story.

> I was nine years old when I first used drugs. I always hung out with older people and felt that I related better to people who were older than me. I was more mature than kids

my own age. One day I was playing basketball at the middle school and my ball missed the basket and rolled down the hill. My friend and I ran after it, and it had stopped next to a group of eighteen- and nineteen-year-olds who we thought were just smoking pot. When we got closer to the group, we saw that they were smoking meth. The oldest guy in the group told us that we had seen too much and needed to smoke some so that we would get in as much trouble as them if we told on them. We told them that we didn't want to, but the older guy got really angry and threatened to hurt us. We smoked it with them and then went to my friend's house, where I had planned on spending the night. We didn't think that the meth had affected us at all. We stayed up the entire night. In the morning we crashed and could not go to school because we were too exhausted. We never told anyone what had happened at the schoolyard. I had no idea that drugs would become a regular part of my life.

The next time that I used drugs was when I was eleven years old and I had a crush on a nineteen-year-old boy. I smoked meth with him and he took advantage of me. That was really bad. I then used drugs anytime that they were available. I rarely had to buy them. The older guys that I hung out with kept me in supply. I've used pot, crystal meth, and heroin. I'm the only child at my house; my brothers and sisters live in other places, so my mom and stepfather have only me to focus on. Sometimes that is why I think that I rebelled as much as I did—so that they couldn't control everything about me.

I first realized that I had a drug problem when I was coming down from being high on meth in juvenile detention, after being arrested for auto theft. I had been partying with a group of friends and we decided that we should steal this car that we knew about. Someone in the group had already taken the keys. We were all high, and it seemed like a good idea. I had just turned thirteen. The entire group of us snuck out of the house and went to the home where the car was located. We didn't want to start the car in the driveway so we rolled it out of the driveway and down the street. We then jumped in and started to drive. Because none of us had any experience with driving a car, our driving wasn't that good and we crossed the middle line a lot. This attracted police attention. We stopped the car and all started running, but I got caught. I was taken to detention, where I spent the next three days. I spent that time sleeping off the effects of the meth and worrying about how much trouble I was going to be in with my parents. I was released to my parents with a court date for later that month. I was now involved with a seventeen-year-old boy. Every morning when I was supposed to be at school, I would be at his house, where we would be smoking meth together. At this point I was still doing okay in school except that my attendance was starting to slip. I always told my parents that I was sick and couldn't go to school because of migraines. One day [my boyfriend] and a friend of his suggested that we go to another town to pick up some drugs. I went along with the understanding that they would get me back home about the time school was out, so that my parents wouldn't suspect anything. I talked a friend into coming along with us. We spent an entire seven hours inside the car smoking and snorting meth after the guys picked it up. When I realized what time it was I knew that I was in trouble, so I decided that I just wouldn't go home. As a result, I spent eight or nine days on the run, staying with adults with drug connections. I would trade babysitting services for drugs and a place to crash. One time I suspected that my stepdad was outside one of the places where I was staying, so I made the kid I was babysitting answer the door while I hid under the bed. As I was hiding out under the bed, I realized that I was laying on something. When I rose up I saw that the items under me were syringes that had been discarded under the bed. I decided to go home.

Jasmine was only twelve when she first witnessed someone shooting heroin, and she was utterly repulsed. Despite the revulsion, though, she herself shot up for the first time just four months later, and quickly assumed that the drug was the solution to all of her problems. It made her feel like Superwoman.

Throughout all of this, Jasmine was in and out of detention centers on approximately thirteen different occasions for a variety of crimes, ranging from auto theft to drug possession. She was also placed in detention for probation violations of curfew, running away from home, and failing her drug tests. This was in part due to her young age; authorities were reluctant to keep a thirteen-year-old locked up with more criminally sophisticated, older adolescents.

Detention was a walk in the park. The first couple of days you are on orientation and basically stay in your room. You can also opt for a sick day so that you get an extra room day. So you have three or four days where you can sober up and sleep. Then, if you are there longer, you just kiss staff's ass and you get privileges. Then I would get out.

I went to one session of the outpatient drug program. I didn't respect the counselors. I believed that I knew more about drug addiction than any of them and I should be running the program. It was a waste of time. I wasn't ready to change. I still believed that I could beat my drug tests. I would calculate my body weight, the amount and type of drugs that I used, and because meth would leave my system fairly quickly, I could then figure out what was the last day of the week that I could use and have it out of my system before my next meeting with my probation counselor.

After numerous probation violations, Jasmine was placed in a longer-term residential treatment program.

I was so angry. I didn't think I needed to be there. I couldn't believe that my probation officer would put me in there. I thought that she was such a bitch. For the first month to month and a half, I fought the program. When I didn't see me getting my way, I thought I would do my usual kiss-ass routine and faking my way through the program. This didn't work, either. When you live at a program, you can't keep the ass-kissing thing up 24/7. Someone, staff or other kids, will eventually piss you off or call you on something and you'll react the way you really are. It took a while, but I finally either gave in or gave up and started sincerely working with the program. After that, things really started turning around for me. I started to see staff differently, my parents differently, and my own behavior differently. I was in the Touchstone program for over nine months. I was so proud at my graduation. The program director, Mike, was actually crying because he was proud of me. He had been there for me so many times. Before I graduated from the program, I went back to my school during the day and would come back to Touchstone at night. The day I went back to school, Mike gave me his cell phone number and told me to call him if I had any problems. In between classes, I ran into an old drug friend of mine who asked if I wanted to get high. When I refused, this person got really snotty and asked me who I thought that I was. She then told me that I was a junkie and would always be a junkie. I turned around and left as soon as I could, but the whole time I was wondering to myself if she wasn't right. I thought about turning back around and getting high again. Thankfully, I remembered Mike's offer and I immediately called him. He told me to stay right where I was and he would come get me immediately. And he did. If he wouldn't have answered his phone or would've told me some bullshit thing about being strong and working through the problem, I wouldn't be here right now. I'd be using or dead. I'd be that junkie that all of my old friends remembered.

Jasmine is on track to finish high school on time. She is attending night school to make sure she can graduate with her class. She also has a part-time job and eventually wants to complete college and work in human services, maybe even become a probation officer.

I really feel the need to give back. So many people helped me get my life and my head together. I know that I have a lot to offer kids who are in similar situations or are thinking that they have all of the answers. I'll be tough but fair. I won't be their friend until they are ready to accept responsibility for their behavior. I always thought that adults that acted like they were my friends were cool. Now I know that if an adult wants to be my friend, they probably don't have my best interests in mind.

I will want to know everything about my kids' life. Where they're going, when they're going to be back, who they're with, and what they'll be doing. I will always be there for them, just like my mom has always been there for me. She didn't give up on me but she didn't want to make the tough calls, because she was afraid of losing me. She knows now that not making the tough calls could've been the reason she would have lost me. We've both learned so much from this. I actually talk to her now instead of telling her what I think that she wants to hear from me. I've learned that disagreeing isn't the worst thing that can happen between us as long as we're honest and open, and I know that I'm the kid and she's the parent.

Since the conclusion of this interview, Jasmine has been living in a foster home. She was involved in a verbal disagreement with her stepfather, who hit her several times and grabbed her arm as she ran away from him, dislocating her shoulder. When the juvenile authorities talked with Jasmine's mother about leaving her husband in order to protect Jasmine, her mother chose to remain with her husband rather than protect her daughter. She reasoned that Jasmine would soon be of legal age and out of the house, thus eliminating the problem. She also felt that her husband was owed some understanding and forgiveness for everything he'd gone through while helping his wife try to get Jasmine straightened out.

Jasmine's story highlights the modern parent's dilemma.

What is the proper balance between being a friend to your child and being a parent? On the one hand, you want to create an environment where your child feels comfortable enough to come to you with all manner of problems. On the other hand, you want to be firm enough to maintain control in order to ensure your child's well-being. Finding this balance is a lifelong challenge.

Jasmine had a number of criminogenic risk factors that, if properly assessed earlier, would have provided juvenile justice workers with a clear indication of the appropriate services to provide and interventions to employ for her. "Criminogenic factors" is a professional term to describe risk factors that drive criminal behavior. These factors included drug and alcohol use, poor peer relations, and academic challenges. As Jasmine pointed out, her young age trumped all of these serious factors when professionals were trying to figure out what to do with her. Their inability to acknowledge that a thirteen-year-old girl could be a serious offender and serious addict allowed precious time to slip away before treatment commenced.

Jasmine's story also highlights the important role that just one caring adult can have in the life of an at-risk child. The fact that the Touchstone program manager, Mike, was there for her was the crucial difference between relapse and sustained recovery.

Chapter 2

Arturo

If you were to meet Arturo today, it's likely you would have to hustle to keep up with him. Art's days are full: At Catholic Community Services, he works full time as supervisor of the Young Fathers program, which is designed to identify and support fathers struggling to meet the needs of their children and families. In this role, Art is part counselor, a bit mentor, and a portion drill instructor. He is both teaching and modeling the skills that will assist these youthful dads in managing their anger, avoiding relapse into addiction, and being present for their children. He also attends Lane Community College, where this term he is enrolled in three classes: Pharmacology, Ethics, and Introduction to Counseling. Art's home life is full: he and his wife, Rachel, are raising three children and have a fourth on the way. Now in his early thirties, Art is determined to make up for lost time.

He was born in Riverside, California, but when we met him, over fifteen years ago, he was already known as "Rocky," a streetwise young man with a history of theft, drug dealing,

and anger management problems that often led to violence. As
Art describes his childhood, he remembers that even his in
utero experience was a difficult one.

> I was born a methadone-addicted baby. My mom was
> drinking while she was on methadone when she was preg-
> nant with me. My mom almost died when I was born, and
> anyways, the relationship between her and my dad was a
> lot of domestic violence, so they split up soon after I was
> born, due to my dad hitting her. And then we went from
> Riverside, California, up to Medford, Oregon, and we con-
> tinuously moved back and forth from there to Riverside.

His mother, wanting something better for her young son
and his older sister, thought that Medford—a small lumber and
farming community in southern Oregon—would be a better
place to raise a family. Art said that Medford was "a lifetime
away from Riverside." Riverside is wedged into the southern
part of the greater Los Angeles area, and is known as the In-
land Empire. It's a community made up mainly of Hispanics
and African Americans, and gangs there are rampant.

At that time, Medford was an almost all white community
of loggers and mill workers. It represented a possible escape
from the torment of drug addiction and domestic violence
Rocky's mother had known with his father. But despite the
move, it was harder to escape the family's ties, not to mention
the forces of her addiction, than his mother imagined.

> Riverside was a very angry place. I remember that from
> growing up in the neighborhoods I was in. As far as being

in a gang or not, you were either with the guys around you or you were against them. It was a really hard place to really get involved with anyone without being peer-pressured into something. And the amazing thing that I noticed there from moving here [to Oregon], too, is the age difference. It started out a lot younger there than when it did here. We were stealing from stores—just candy; we were just kids. We were like six, seven, or eight years old, but we were able to go wherever we wanted, because our parents were usually using or drinking. So we'd go to the stores and we'd steal candy, and then we'd go to the park and eat the candy or we'd go to Target or something and steal GI Joes, or whatever toy we wanted, and we'd play with the toys at the park, and just hang out.

I remember hanging out until all hours of the night before I'd come home, because I just didn't want to go home. My mom quit using heroin and she got off the methadone, but then she got real heavy into drinking, and the boyfriends she ended up getting were usually heavy drinkers as well. And I just remember, if he wasn't hitting on my mom, he was hitting me or my sister. The abuse escalated. It seems like she would drop one guy and get a worse one when the first guy stopped coming around. By the time I was nine years old it got so bad I couldn't live there anymore, and either my family or the authorities sent me to San Pedro, to my aunt's. So when I was nine I went to San Pedro and they saw the bruises and everything, and that was it. They took me to court and filed child abuse against my mom and we went to trial. It was actually in the newspapers in Medford, Oregon, when this happened. I think that was my breaking point. After I had told the court everything that was going on in the house with my mom and my sister, it came to their turn, and my mom had hooked up with the guy again, and they both pretty much told the court that I was lying and they didn't want me anyway.

As juvenile counselors in juvenile probation departments, we always tell young people that when facing a judge, they should tell the truth, promising them that this honesty will ensure their safety and protect them and their families from continued abuse, neglect, or addiction in their homes. But in Art's case, he told the truth in court and was punished for it.

Now—this is at nine years old—my mom and my sister were the only people that were that close to me, and I felt like there was something the matter with me. I felt worthless. The abuse was one thing, but I think that the trial really did it. So I went to San Pedro and I lived there from nine years old until I was eleven, at my aunt and uncle's, who were really good people, World War II veterans. You know the World War II story: you get married, my uncle went to war, he came back, he got a job, they built the house, and they're still living in it to this day. The whole Ozzie and Harriet thing.

They put me in Catholic school, and Catholic school down there is a lot different from up here. I went to school with Slovakians, Italians, Greeks, and Mexicans, and one thing that they all liked to do was fight, and our parents would allow us to fight, so I was just this skinny little kid with these big bottle cap welfare glasses that they handed out in the eighties. I don't know if you remember those, but they were pretty big, so I was pretty much a target, and I went back and forth, getting in trouble and getting in fights. They nicknamed me Rocky because even the fights I won, it looked like I lost, because I was really small.

I became sexually active around that same time, trying to get up on girls, already having that desire at that young age. And I became too much of a problem for my aunt and uncle. They didn't know what to do with me. I also was suicidal, had made two attempts to take my life. And I was seeing a nun who was also a psychiatrist, and that didn't go over too well, either. So they moved me up here to Eugene, Oregon, with my dad and my uncle.

My dad and my uncle are heroin addicts. They call them *Degatos*, and the term *OG* [original gangster] would relate to my dad and my uncle. They started out in the sixties: CYA, Tracy, Chino, San Quentin, Folsom; and that's where they grew up. I had a cousin that was three years older than I was, and I think it was the second night I got here to Eugene—I was always this outcast in San Pedro—and the second night I got to Eugene, my cousin, who was probably about fourteen or fifteen, throws a garage party. He hands me a bottle of Old English and tells one of these girls that she's going to take care of me that night. Here I am about eleven and I'm going to turn twelve and my cousin's just this idol to me. He had girls, he was selling dope for my uncle, he was already drinking at the house, he was a good fighter, and I just felt like I had made it. I was finally home. I was accepted. And I idolized that; he became my idol, not just my cousin, but my dad and my uncle.

Our bedtime stories at night would be my dad or my uncle nodding out smoking weed and drinking Old English, talking about what the old days were like in San Quentin or Folsom. I thought that was the coolest thing to do. How cool is it? And the way that I saw people treat them—treated them with so much respect. They would do anything for them. And I wanted that, and my uncle put me to work, and I started selling. First I started selling weed, and then meth, and then I graduated to heroin. I think it was when I was twelve when I got busted on my first burglary. I robbed this kid's house and I went to juvenile hall, a place called Skipworth Detention Center. I met my juvenile counselor and my multicultural worker. They were trying to help me, and since they knew my dad and my uncle, they were trying to break the cycle with me. And all I saw was another way I could maybe manipulate the system.

So when I got out, obviously, nothing had changed. As soon as I got out, my uncle gave me some dope to sell, and my older cousin gave me a girl, and it was like a graduation party when I got out. Because of what I was doing, I kept on getting incarcerated. And what I found out, when I got incarcerated, was that I didn't have a stable life out there, and I was kind of competing with my dad and my uncle and my cousin. But when I was in juvenile hall, because I was getting trained by my father, uncle, and cousin to be a soldier in the family gang, the guys I was locked up with in Skipworth really were nowhere close to my level, to what I had already learned. It gave me a feeling of importance, trying to get over on the system, trying to run the area, and the power and control that came with it when people would do what I said. And my dad and my uncle didn't help. My dad was smuggling me in weed in balloons. He put weed in one balloon or two balloons, and then in another balloon he put the rolling papers, and in another balloon he put the matchstick heads with the little match strip on it. My dad slipped it to me during contact visits. I then swallowed the balloons and would later shit them out in my room, into my pillowcase. And that pretty much went on every time I was incarcerated. But I finally got busted; someone told on me, and all they found was a pillowcase full of shit in my cell. And I remember when the guards were going through it, I got the sick feeling that I knew they weren't going to find anything, and then they put me on red flag. It was called red flag, and that's when I didn't get to go to school. I wasn't able to do anything.

And instead of making me think about what choices I had made to put me in that position, instead I started thinking about another graduation, like I was doing something by keeping my mouth shut, like I was following the code that was being taught to me. My dad taught me that. I remember when I was about eleven or twelve years old, when I first moved here, he would take me as cover to go with him into stores and he would just jack. He'd have this trench coat on and he would just put, I don't know, eight pairs of Levis, the really expensive ones, and silk shirts, and just put them under the trench coat and put his arm down like this, to hold it, and then he would hold my hand and we'd walk out. My first charge, when I first moved here, was I got caught shoplifting from Albertsons. We didn't have any food or anything, and I told my dad, "Let's get some food." And he said, "If you want food, go get it yourself." So I put bacon underneath my shirt, and I put chorizo under my armpit. And I had all this stuff, and I'm thinking I'm slick and I walk out of that Albertsons—it's the one right by the employment department—and they busted me. And I remember then, they hit me up. They said, "We know your dad knows; we saw you." They have those two-way mirrors, and they're looking at me in the aisle while I'm doing it, and my dad's standing right there. "So just let us know and nothing is going to happen. We just to need to know the truth." And I still wouldn't tell on him. I just wouldn't do it. I guess the best part is I always wanted to be accepted by my dad, and when I did that—keep my mouth shut or follow any of the other rules that they taught us—I got that look of approval, of my dad being proud of me. My dad being proud and the look of approval is what fed me and kept me going. The worst part of it was the fact that it was only momentary; you were only as good as your last deed. Later on that day I could do something, not stupid, but just something that a kid does, and I would get that look of disappointment again, and then I'd have to do something again to try to see acceptance. I think that was the biggest part that led me into this, the striving to be accepted by someone, but they were always the wrong people. But I ended up getting a probation officer, and with his and another counselor's help, they would always talk about opportunities in life, and say that the possibilities weren't just for certain people, that they were for everyone. When I saw good people like that, it opened the door to talk to them—trusting them a little. They seemed like more than just people in the system. They seemed like people who cared about me. But there were other people who were against me. They told me I wasn't going to amount to shit, that I was no different than my dad or my uncle. And I remember what that did to me. It showed me that they were against me. Seeing me like that showed me that they felt they were on one side and I was on the other—and they thought my side was shit. It was just negative reinforcement—I already saw them as part of the system, and when they forced that message on me, it showed me they really were not on my side. It said, "Okay, you're my enemy." And I'm not going to team up with that or look at that as something that's supposed to help me. That was a lot different than the other people I encountered. The good people in the system that were telling me that I could go to school, that I could graduate, that there were things I could do. They were still part of that system, but I could see that they wanted to help me, and I could open the door to that.

Judge Ann was like that. I remember she took me under her wing, and I hung out with her. We went to a forum that was about the Measure 11 thing together. [Measure 11 is a mandatory sentencing law passed by the Oregon voter initiative process in 1994. It significantly increased sentences for person-to-person felony cases. These are crimes against individuals instead of property.] I remember they were talking about Measure 11 and what they were going to do about mandatory sentences, even for juveniles. And I remember standing up and saying, "Hey, that kid you guys are talking about is me." I remember that I had an impact when I had said that, and it felt good to be a part of something. I'd always wanted to do something, but I never thought that I could. It really helped me out a lot when the people in the system told me I could do something.

Anyway, when I got caught for shitting in my pillow, I wouldn't tell on my dad, I wouldn't say anything, and I had been on red flag for a long period of time. The multicultural counselor finally went to someone and said, "Hey, you know, part of his culture is not to tell, and he's never going to tell, and you can't leave him here." And so I got out, and then I hit the kid that told on me, and they put me back on red flag. And after, because of what had happened with my dad, they didn't want to put me back in my family's care anymore, so they put me in a Christian Family Services shelter home. I remember I had—I think it was my fourteenth—a birthday out there at CFS, because I remember two staff took me shopping for clothes, and they took me out to eat. It's Daniel's now, but it used to be called something else, right across from the mission. I remember the feeling of gratitude that came over me, because with everything I had done, they loved unconditionally. It might have been professional on their part, but for me that was one thing that I never had. When I got to be too much of a problem for my uncle and for my aunt, they would send me away. When I became too much of a problem for my dad and my uncle, they would send me away. When I'd cause too much problems for my mom, they'd send me away. So, that was pretty much my idea of relationships: I'm going to push you to your limits so that you can push me away so it reaffirms that no one really cares. I didn't have that with these adults. They were pretty solid in trying to help me. They ended up putting me in Looking Glass or Stepping Stones—it was by the University of Oregon—and they had put this guy in there, and he was a pedophile. I think he molested his two-year-old sister or something. I met him when we were in Skipworth, so when I saw him there that night, I beat him up and I told him not to say anything, and he ended up telling on me.

Art was subsequently ordered by the juvenile court judge to be placed in Stepping Stone Lodge, a residential treatment facility. While he was there, he and his father participated in an intake interview.

My dad had used before coming, and kept nodding off during the interview. He didn't use it to get high, just enough to stay well during the interview. He never was dishonest about it. He was a heroin addict. I'm sure he was doing all kinds of illegal stuff, and I'm not saying he wasn't doing that, but he didn't present it like, "Hey, I don't know what you're talking about." He knew what was going on at that meeting. But he was an addict. And he did a lot of things you might not do, to get money for drugs. He didn't have any furniture in the house because he'd sell anything he had for heroin. I remember every time I'd get locked up, he would rent out my room to one of the connections. And then when I would get out, I would have to find somewhere else to stay. One time we were living right there by the entrance to the elementary school, and he had the room, and then there was this other room that was mine, and I went to juvie. When I got out he had rented out to some border brothers that were selling heroin, so he put a couch in the kitchen. It was the kind of couch that collapsed—the back end falls back, and it had springs sticking out—and that was my room. We didn't cook. Top Ramen. I knew how to make burritos before I even went to jail, the Top Ramen burritos, because that's what we kind of grew up on. "Border brothers" is what we call the guys that are from Mexico. It's disrespectful to say "wetback" or "spic." "Border brothers" is more of a respectful manner, of acknowledging that we are related in some form, but that there is a separation there, too, to a certain limit. Chicano is a Mexican American, which identifies us as being one of them, them being one of us. It is a different culture in itself. It's a totally different culture. But that's how we labeled each other. It's funny how we complain about people profiling us, but yet we profile each other.

I didn't want to join a gang. That's how my dad and my uncle raised us. They both had opportunities to get in the Mexican Mafia, and my uncle Bobby, who was the oldest out of the others, told my uncle Vic and my dad to never do that because you'll end up doing someone else's work and not getting paid for it. So the family had their own little thing, and that was our gang. It was our family. It was me, my cousin, and my dad and my uncle—that was our gang. If someone ripped us off . . . I remember this guy JJ got a pound of weed on credit from my cousin Johnny, and said that he got jacked and no longer had it. So me and my dad and my uncle and my cousin went over to the guy's house and took everything out of his house: his TV, his stereos. We took everything and we told him he still owed us the money. And he did pay, and then we gave some of the stuff back. There was no reason for me to be gang affiliated when I was here with my family, because that was our protection, each other.

Despite treatment interventions, Art's life continued to spiral out of control. Still under the strong influences of his family, and motivated by a desire to be accepted and earn status and respect, he began running drugs between California and Oregon with his family's full knowledge and encouragement.

I would get out of juvie and then I would go to California, and then I would come back, and then I'd go to juvie, and then I'd go to California, and then I'd come back. During those times when I'd go down there, my mom lived in Riverside and she was selling large amounts of methamphetamine. Bricks. And some of the guys that she had coming over were affiliated. I had never become a part of the gang, but I became what is called an associate. I was just a friend of theirs. If something went down, I had to help them. Or if I needed help, I could ask them for help. And the whole reason for that is because at Ramona in the nineties, they already had—what are those things you walk through in the court—metal detectors. We had metal detectors in our school already. This was at Ramona and Poly High School in Riverside. Palm Springs didn't have any; it was pretty nice. When I was there you had to be associated with someone if you were doing anything illegal, so that there was cover there for you. When I was in San Pedro, I hung out with the guys from Rancho San Pedro. When I was in Riverside, I was hanging out with a gang. In Moreno Valley, I was hanging out with another gang. And in Palm Springs, I was only there about three or four months—what were they called? Something Locos. I was only there for a little bit. It just seemed like I was attracted to that kind of crowd. Those were the people I got along with. If you were going to do anything illegal, then a part of it is playing with the gangs. It's kind of like taxes. It is. If you want to work and do that, you have to pay taxes. Down there it's kind of seen as the same thing. If you're doing something illegal and you're making money off of it, or you're involved with something and making money off of it, and you're not paying the local gang in your area, then you get charged a tax. You get a warning, and then you get a beating, and then they can put a mark on you, and that could be anywhere from beating on sight to terminate. I was

> hanging out with them more as friends, and just partying
> with them. When I was down there I really wasn't selling
> anything. I boosted clothes and stuff because I liked nice
> clothes, but we didn't have much money, not that my
> mom would give me any.

Art had one uncle who had been in the Merchant Marine.
He agreed to take Art into his home, but with one condition:
Art's father wouldn't be allowed to visit or have any contact
with him. Despite two generations of struggle with the family,
Art's uncle was willing to give him an opportunity to live in
the affluence of Palm Springs. Despite his successes in life,
Art's uncle had been rejected by the family because he was in
an openly gay relationship.

> He was living in Canoga Park, but he bought the house in
> Palm Springs because he didn't want me living in Canoga
> Park because it's a pretty bad area. He went into the Mer-
> chant Marines during World War II, and then after that
> he bought an upholstery shop in Hollywood. Then he
> bought another upholstery shop in Venice Beach, and he
> became very successful. He's definitely strong-minded.
> His partner, Uncle Allen—they were together for over
> thirty years. They were old school. They were definitely
> old school with the rules and how things were supposed
> to be. There was really no "Come on, Art, you can do it."
> It was: "You need to pull your head out of your ass and do
> what you're supposed to." See, my uncle Tito really took
> after my grandfather. You work hard and you don't com-
> plain. It's all you do. As a man, that's what you're sup-
> posed to do. And even though he was gay, he was a man's

man. He taught me a little bit about work ethic. I appreciate that because that helped me out a lot when they treated me like a man. They didn't treat me like a kid; they treated me like a man, and they really raised the bar for me. Because what I noticed, when people don't raise the bar for me, I manipulate them. But when people raise the bar for me, it challenges me and I try to succeed. My uncle Tito isn't alive, but I still have contact with Uncle Allen. I e-mail him; we e-mail each other. He doesn't like talking on the phone much. I told him how much clean time I had, and he said that ain't shit—he's got twenty-eight years. He said that when I get ten years, then maybe I'll stick around. He is proud of me, but he told me not to get a big head over a couple of years, that it still ain't shit.

The change in living conditions and expectations was dramatic, but Art continued down the path of criminality. His opportunity for turnaround dissolved in less than two months.

After I left Palm Springs, I didn't want to go back to juvie because I thought I'd be locked up. So I stayed at Colorado Springs, and I waited for the next plane to come, and then I went back. Then I got into some more trouble with my dad—I ripped off his connection—and then after that we got raided. That's when my cousin and I were taken into foster custody, and we went back to my aunt and uncle's. They told me that if I were to live there, I had to either go to school or work, so I got a job at Vons and I actually worked forty hours a week, sometimes sixty hours a week, especially around Christmas. I think I was about seventeen at the time, sixteen or seventeen.

Art returned to Oregon and the chaotic criminal life of his father, uncle, and cousin Johnny. The criminal lifestyle is ingrained in most of Art's family, not just in his mother and father. Art can recite other family members' criminal accomplishments, and in those accounts, he gives examples of how his family experienced loyalty, commitment, and support. These family ties might be difficult to understand, to acknowledge as a "good thing," because they exist in the context of criminal activity and even abusive lifestyles. But the importance of family is evident with Art.

My uncle Bobby was the leader of the pack. He was the one that started everything. Bobby was pretty much a zoot suiter back in the day. Back in the zoot suit riots— remember those?—he was the zoot suiter. My uncle Victor was the pachuco, which was like the next level; that came after the zoot suiters. And then my dad was labeled a *chollo*, which came after the pachucos. I wonder why me and my cousin Johnny have had such separate lives. Right now he's in California State Prison. He's been at Chino and Vacaville, and he's been at OSP and Snake River. And I'm wondering: What was the difference? I think the difference was, for me, that I had time with my Niña and Niño. They taught me some good things. I had people like my probation officer and my counselor. And whether I heard it at that time or heard it later on, I was open to some good things. I lived with my uncle Tito and my uncle Allen, and they taught me some good things. I had positive people in my life, so it wasn't all bad. My cousin never had anything except Vic, and it really, for me, couldn't get any uglier than that.

I guess, through the life that I have today, I've done a

lot of work in treatment. I've done a lot of work in the twelve-step community. I've done a lot of crying. I've done a lot of paperwork. I've started to heal. And I think that's why I'm able to identify it as my life and not who I was. Those are my family members, but that's not who I am. Before, when I'd tell a story, anger would come up, or sadness, or different emotions, and they still do a little bit, but not as much, because I'm able to separate it from who I am today. When people told me what I was doing was wrong, that automatically put me on the defensive, and after that I usually discounted everything they had to say. That's why I related so much to my counselor, because I felt that she understood the culture and the lifestyle that I was living. Instead of saying it was wrong, they said I could do something different. In that aspect, it's not really a negative thing. They're just saying, "It is the way it is, but you can do something different." Rather than coming right off the bat and telling me, "You're wrong. The way you live is wrong." Because as a kid, that's all I knew, and the last thing I wanted to know is that it was wrong. You want to tell me that I have options—I like that idea, I'm always open for options. But to tell me that I'm a bad person, or I'm a bad kid, or that I have a bad family or a bad life, I'll discount anything that person has to say afterward.

Art's wife is also a recovering drug addict, and they have defied the odds by staying together. While they did get lost in their addictions for a while, both Art and his wife found a way to deal with the demands of recovery, parenting, work, etc., and build a better life for their children. Both feel strongly that their drug, alcohol, and criminal experiences give them the perspective necessary to help others confront their own addictions and struggles. Art maintains contact with his father, but limits his children's interaction with their grandfather. Art also stays in contact with Judge Ann, who is now a federal court judge. Art is a regular visitor to her court, speaking of his own recovery and working with young men in the role of sponsor.

Chapter 3

Rachel

Rachel is a petite woman in her early thirties. She has an easy smile and an engaging manner. She is also a former client of ours, and we remember the difficulties she faced while going back and forth between home placement and treatment centers. This recollection of Rachel stands in stark contrast to the young woman sitting before us today. The anger that used to be her constant companion has turned to compassion and understanding. The defensive shield that she wore has given way to a self-assured, nurturing aura. Gone are the edginess and aggression. Now Rachel is determined to make a better life for herself and her children. She also feels a calling to give of herself to help others.

At first Rachel wasn't sure why we wanted to interview her for this book. "My story is extremely different than my husband's, I grew up in a middle-class family with two parents. I am married to a man who came from poverty and whose family struggled with drug abuse and domestic violence," she reminded us. She was referring to her view, shared by many of the professionals she has met over the years, that her criminality could be directly linked to the sexual abuse she suffered. She was both the victim of abuse and a perpetrator of it, as her story will describe. It's what she learned; it's what she did. But as is the case for most of the people you'll read about, nothing is ever that simple. Her story demonstrates that while the system is capable of helping, it's also capable of making situations worse. And her story is perhaps one of the best for busting the myth of peer pressure. When teens begin smoking cigarettes, drinking, using illegal drugs, getting pregnant, and even committing crimes, peer pressure is routinely blamed. It evokes images of vulnerable children being forced to do something they wouldn't otherwise do, of intimidating and manipulative teenagers threatening vulnerable peers with harm if their behaviors aren't mimicked. But this is a myth.

At-risk youths are particularly vulnerable to a different kind of pressure, one that arises from desperation and loneliness. It is a hunger to be included, involved, and connected. That hunger pushes them to connect with anyone who will have them. They often identify as long-term friends people they've known for only days or weeks. Many find themselves involved with adults or other adolescents who prey on this hunger and exploit their desire to be connected and included. The overt nature of peer pressure is lacking in this scenario, but the results are the same.

The hunger itself is a healthy thing; the need to connect and to feel a sense of belonging is appropriate at this stage in an adolescent's development. The challenge, for each child, is to make the right connection at the right time, and with the right person. Rather than connecting with a drug dealer or the users who spend the bulk of their time in a crack house, an at-risk child would be much better off connecting with a youth group, an employer, a mentor, or a teacher, so he could learn to address his problems appropriately and avoid putting his safety in jeopardy. To those of us providing treatment, this hunger can be used to help connect with these children.

Teens' attraction to negative peers is based on their own internal pressure to belong. The mythical external extortion from peers is actually an internal raging need to be part of something that separates them from their families and aligns them with people who make them feel like "somebody." Adolescence is a time when young adults make strides in gaining independence from parents, and when connections with other young adults become more important. As a result, some adolescents end up choosing to do things they might not feel compelled to do if they weren't driven by their own need to belong. For many adolescents, this need is stronger than the common sense they've demonstrated until this point in their lives.

For Rachel, needing to belong was more than an exercise in myth and reality. It was her life. Her childhood keepsake was the pain of being sexually abused by her stepfather while emotionally and physically abandoned by her mother—a pain numbed only by drugs and sex during her teen years. Then the system charged with protecting her from harm in her own home created the best possible place for her to be abused by delinquent youths. But she didn't call it abuse. She called it belonging.

My parents were divorced and at that time I was an only child. My mother parented in a very relaxed way. Her style was "Go run wild and naked—have fun." There was no heavy discipline. I was pretty spoiled. Then Mom married my stepfather when I was four, and everything changed. When he stepped in, it went totally opposite. He was very strict, and I didn't speak unless spoken to. My mother was going back to working on a business degree. And after school, she was working all the time, doing all this stuff. So I was either with day care or with my stepfather, because he didn't work. He was very abusive to me. And he was a really heavy alcoholic. So it was kind of difficult as a child growing up in that. There was a lot of tension in the house.

Mom's best defense has always been denial. The way she grew up was also very different than this. Her father loved her and her sisters. They were spoiled just like I was in the beginning. My mother told me one time she wanted to paint her room red. Her dad said okay. It was like those kinds of things. So she grew up letting children be children, and my stepfather grew up very strict. It was really different; he grew up very poor. He had his own issues. I don't really know what was wrong with him, other than he was an alcoholic and was extremely abusive.

My mom ended up getting pregnant, and I had a little brother come into the picture; we moved a lot, and then my mom got pregnant with my little sister. Because I was the stepdaughter, I wasn't favored. My little brother was the pride and joy. It has nothing to do with my brother, because me and my brother are very close now, but he rubbed it in my face a lot. It was expected that I didn't go to friends' houses. I was not allowed to spend the night at people's houses or have them spend the night with us. It was all very close, a connected family. I believe today that it was like that because of the abuse that was going on.

When my little sister was born, we moved to another state. Through the years of the moving and going back and forth, the abuse continually got worse. When I was in middle school and I was starting to develop as a young woman, the abuse got worse, a lot worse. My friends started noticing bruises on me and dragged me down to the counseling office at the school, and that's when a lot came out.

There was a lot of sexual abuse going on. Now that I've been in counseling and really able to live through some things, and I guess now that I'm older and my brain is able to cope with stuff, I can talk about it.

When all the sexual abuse was brought up, I did have charges brought against me for sexually abusing my brother. My brother also remembered things; there was forced sexual abuse between the two of us. It's kind of hard to explain that part; this is something I've just dealt with in the last year. So, with all that coming up, even though she knew about the abuse and everything, my mother stayed with my stepfather, and I went to a shelter at that time. I was there a pretty long time and I actually liked it. I remember my mom trying to leave my stepfather, but she always went back.

Before the sex abuse charges were brought against Rachel for abusing her brother, she was placed in a foster shelter, a residential treatment facility for youths who are victims of abuse. Rachel was placed in the shelter for reasons of protection and safety. With her stepfather still in the house, it was much too dangerous for her to remain there. The shelter she was sent to, however, contained a mix of youths. Some were like Rachel and needed a safe place to live. But others were there because they were delinquent. Despite the inherent dangers of mixing these populations, many state and local jurisdictions develop these commingling treatment facilities because limited budgets do not allow for operating different facilities for the two types of youth.

I loved being at the shelter. It got me away from a very bad situation. But I really didn't know about drugs, and I was living with people who had drug problems, so I learned about smoking pot and [taking] acid from them. The shelter had two sides. One for boys, and one for girls. I was already pretty well introduced to the careless needs of young men. I learned that boys could give me what I needed. I got a lot of attention from them because I was young. I was younger than most of the other kids in there; there were only a few kids about my age, thirteen or fourteen years old. It seemed like the other kids there were sixteen; they were older, and they were runaways and they were brawlers. They were fighting. They came from my background of abuse, but we had a nice house, we had nice cars. These kids didn't grow up like that. I came from the nice neighborhood and they didn't. And these kids at the shelter accepted me. When I was at my neighborhood, I wasn't accepted by those kids, because no one understood the abuse that I was going through. But these kids, they went through it, and so it was all good.

I learned a different way of dealing with my anger. I learned that it was okay to yell and shout like the other kids. I learned to be very aggressive. At that time that's what I felt was okay because that's what I saw other people doing. It was okay to hit things, it was okay to throw things. I remember this girl stole something. We went down to the city pool and this girl stole some shoes, and I was the one who got called in the office. The other kids were telling me, "You better keep your mouth shut, we don't rat on each other. You better keep your mouth shut, you better not say anything." And the funny thing is, I'm the one who didn't rat out. I was so terrified of these kids that I would not. I said, "I don't know, I didn't see anything." I was so terrified that these kids who grew up the way they did would be the ones that would spill the beans. These are guidelines, this is a way of living, and I really took that seriously.

I don't remember my parents coming to see me while I was at the shelter. I don't remember my mom coming to see me. I wanted . . . well, it was hard.

When I left the shelter, I learned to hang out downtown. I learned that you can do all this kind of stuff with them. I learned where all the kids hung out. I went to live with my friend's parents. They even went through something official to get approved for me to live there. The daughter of my parents' friends was my best friend. But I didn't know that her brother was friends with guys I met and that I was really attracted to. They were these guys that were involved with some major illegal activity, and they liked me. I had this power over them, and my friend didn't like that. It caused a lot of problems. So, I moved out of that house shortly after that. I went just to around the corner to another place to live so I could still see the guys.

I started drinking a lot then, running away a lot. I got charged for a theft. I got sent up to Montana, to my dad. This is my biological father that I really hadn't ever had contact with. I got moved into a family that was different, they were well adjusted. I wasn't. They didn't have a lot of money, but they were happy. It was okay for kids to throw a fit, and they didn't get hit. But I was a screwed-up kid by then. I had a lot of abandonment issues, and here's a man that I didn't know for most of my life and all of a sudden I'm supposed to call him Dad. And I got two sisters, and I got a brother, and I got a stepmom, and I'm supposed to think that they all care about me? B.S. I didn't believe it, and I just kept on acting out. So I started really smoking pot. Back then it just made me feel better about myself. For a moment I was someone different. For a moment I was not trying to get attention somehow, trying to get love somehow. I didn't care that my mom, once again, sent me up to a father who had already abandoned me. I really hadn't started therapy with the sexual abuse, so a lot of that was haunting me. I was still living with a lot of the verbal and emotional abuse that was going on, and that was it, that was the ticket: to drink and just forget, just smoke some pot and forget. And all the cool people did that. They looked a lot cooler than me, and it just seemed like they were also the ones that accepted me. They got it; they understood what I was going through. I could relate to them, and they weren't judgmental of who I was, or what I had been through. It was a way of life.

I was so starved for attention. I just wanted to have friends. And, like I said, for a long time I had been kept out of that. I'd been kept away from having friends. All I had known was this abusive family. And then I started meeting other juveniles, and they said, "Come and do this." My first experience of having friends was at the shelter, kids that had problems just like me. Where we lived was not a bad area, but where we went to school was not good. I always thought that was in the movies—the metal detectors—but no, that's real. We had our little gangs where I lived with Mom, but where my dad lived—that's real. And they accepted me. Because I had started knowing how to fight, I learned how to deal with my anger in a different way. It wasn't closed in on me anymore; it erupted on other people. You piss me off, I was going to take all that hatred I had for myself and everybody else and put it on you. And I felt good about it.

I think God liked me. I didn't get caught, I just didn't get caught. I had a theft, and they knew I was a screwed-up kid, so I was going to all this counseling stuff. But I kind of stayed under the radar. I was hanging out with Chicanos or blacks, and I was this sweet, little, innocent white girl. Who was going to look at me? They were getting caught, but I wasn't.

Rachel's mother, who, when the abuse first came to light, chose to stay with the man who'd abused Rachel and her other children, did eventually decide to leave him, but it didn't make for an immediate happy ending for Rachel.

When I was going to these houses to live, after the shelter, my mom was separated from my stepfather, but she didn't want me back. That hurt a lot. I had serious abandonment issues, and, like I said, I had learned to start covering that up. When I moved up to Montana, my mother moved to Nevada, and she had divorced my stepfather. The man she's married to now, I like.

I started going to therapy, but I didn't think it helped. They didn't understand my situation. They would analyze me and do these assessments, and I would read over the assessments and think, "You guys have absolutely no clue who I am." They were already like making decisions on who I was going to be, and what I was going to do, and how I was going to turn out. With these analyses, I was screwed either way. This one guy, a treatment counselor here, told my mom before I moved to Washington, "Either she's going to be a lesbian or she's going to be promiscuous." My mother held my hand and told me it would be okay if I was gay. She didn't say it would be okay if I was promiscuous. I took that one and thought, "Okay, it's okay if I'm gay, but it's not okay if I'm promiscuous, so this is what I'm going to do to hurt you." That's what they were like. They were tossing all these things out there. You met with me three times and I really haven't opened up and talked to you, but you can already sense all that? That's why it was always hard for me with psych evaluations. I'm just looking at them, thinking, "You meet with me for six hours and you've got it all figured out?" I just don't understand that. So I didn't open up. I just told them what they wanted to hear. "Oh, yeah, I was really bad." "Yeah, I had dreams about what happened to me." "Yeah, I disassociate." "Yeah, I'm really screwed up." I just fed them kind of what they wanted to hear. But what I didn't tell them was that I didn't remember a lot of stuff that had happened, and I was having nightmares, and I was depressed, and I was suicidal. I wouldn't tell them that because I was so scared they would lock me up in an institution because that's what I saw would happen to me. I would feed them the top layers of stuff. I wouldn't tell them the panic attacks and anxiety, and how much I was drinking and using, and how much I was being sexually active, to take away that pain. I went through counseling, but I didn't use it to my benefit, because I was terrified. I had a lot of trust issues.

Bill was the first court-appointed attorney I ever had. He became my attorney right when I got involved with the courts. He intimidated me because I didn't understand any of this, but he was always really soft-spoken to me. "Check it out, this is what's going on, this is what's going to happen." And he was always very honest with me, and he told me what I needed to do. He always was really honest. "You can do this, and this is what's going to happen, or you can do this, and this is what's going to happen." He was always really up front with me, and I never had that. But we also had conversations. As I got older and into more trouble, he told me that he knew my history with my family, and he said it was a really shitty hand of cards that I got. That's pretty much what he said. It wasn't fair to me, the parents that I had received. He knew there was something better for me. I just had to make different decisions. He was always a friend; he was my lawyer, but he could talk to me. He was always very honest and he understood. I've had a few professionals come into my life that I really felt like they understood what I was talking about and what I've been through. It wasn't so much that they just read my file and thought, "Okay, she's a screwed-up kid." No, there were reasons why I was screwed up. There were reasons that some of the system failed me in some regard. Even as I got older, and I got into my own trouble as an adult, it was nice to hear, "Yeah, the system failed you, Rachel."

The most obvious way in which the system failed Rachel is that despite all of the alleged sexual abuse, her stepfather was never charged with a crime. From society's viewpoint, if convicted of such heinous acts he should obviously be punished for what he's done, but the trial and sentencing process is also important for the victim, offering the possibility for closure to traumatic events.

It would be charming if we could say that Rachel grew out of her tormented teen years by ending her challenges with drugs, sex, and criminality. But the pain of her childhood didn't stop there. Instead, it followed her into an abusive mar-

riage in her early adult life. She was pregnant for the first time
when she was seventeen. Then she and Tim married when she
was in her twenties, and they had two children together by the
time she was twenty-six.

I know I love him. No matter what me and my husband
went through, there was one thing that we always had in
common: we were both birds with broken wings, and we
could lean on each other, we could fly, so we were very
codependent on each other.

Tim had, in the beginning, a lot of flaws, but there's
one thing that he did through it all—he took care of me.
I always had whatever I needed or wanted, my children
always had whatever they needed and wanted. We didn't
move a lot. He took care of the bills. He took care of me
no matter what. And it wasn't like that before we met.
Then, I was having to hustle. I was having to use my body
to make ends meet. I used my body to get drugs and alcohol. And he gave me a way out of that. I didn't have to be
the hustler anymore. I was taken care of, and I never had
that.

So that part was good. But other parts weren't. When
we were together in the early part, he was abusive, I was
abusive, we were involved with drugs. I was using methamphetamines and heroin. We were heavy users then.

Then I had my kids removed; we had our kids removed. They went to the foster system. The first couple
of times, they went to my mom's house. There were stip-
ulations, like if I could get the house clean, or if I could
get through some type of treatment service, parenting
service, then I would get my kids. So they were never really placed in foster care. My mom just kind of took them.

But then Tim was in jail; I just couldn't pull it together. I could not do it. I couldn't parent on drugs, and I couldn't parent off drugs. So I said, screw it, and they came and got the kids. There was a time that I was trying to hide them out and stuff, because of my fear of the system.

Bill continued to act as her attorney when she entered the adult system. His honesty and direct manner gave Rachel something that few other adults had ever offered her, and in fact, many of them actually took it away: trust. It ushered in one of the most significant decisions of her life.

Bill went through all of this with me. Probably the best way to know someone is through court. He's always been the one person who was straight up with me, honest with me, but never gave up on me. He had to continue helping me even when I got involved in the adult system. He was my lawyer, but he was more than that. One thing he told me when I was in court and I was screwed up—I wasn't getting my kids unless I did the stuff the court told me I had to do, get treatment. He told me, "This will be the hardest thing you ever did in your life." And I looked at him and said, "No, it's not." He told me it would be harder than birth, the hardest thing I've ever done in my life, but the most rewarding.

He was right, definitely right. I wish there was more men like him. I just happen to know all the bad ones.

They always talk about this moment. You get these moments of clarity, and it got me. It hit me that if I didn't stop now, that I was never going to stop and I was never going to see my kids again, and how dare I do that to them when I swore I wouldn't. When everything I had sworn I wouldn't be was what I was doing. I had already emotionally abandoned them, but to completely abandon them like I had been, I just refused to do that, so I went to treatment.

It wasn't the dangers of prostitution or serious drug use that woke Rachel from the nightmare of her childhood pain. Nor was it the physical harm of an abusive relationship with her husband, Tim. Rachel's "moment" didn't arrive from her questioning the violence that had damaged her own life. It came from watching herself get closer to her mother's legacy of abandonment. And in that awareness, she birthed an intolerance of passing that pain on to her own children. What started as a means to get her children back broadened into caring for a hurt that had attached itself to her so many years before. And in caring for it, she changed her relationship with herself first, and then with her kids and her husband. Treatment for drugs and alcohol gave Rachel many of these gifts. The first of which was meeting another adult she would learn to trust.

It was when I was older that I finally opened up to a counselor I worked with. I was able to do that because he was an addict, and I was an addict. He was open to me about that and just shared that with me. It wasn't just something he learned in a textbook. He really did it, he really knew what it was like for me, he knew what it's like to use drugs. He got it.

He was really open to me, and you know what was the coolest thing he told me? He said, "Even though you're a minor, and what's said in this session I have to report to

your PO [parole officer], I don't really have to report anything to your mother." And I thought, "I like you, you're
awesome." It was the first time someone told me what
they would and would not do. Sure, reporting some
things to my PO would have to happen, but it didn't mean
reporting everything. I could just be me. And I was older
by then, and still I had gotten into trouble. But I was all
ready to pay attention to what was in me—what was caus-
ing all these problems. I think there was a part of me that
had a moment of clarity, and I was desperate to see if there
was something different. I think I was ready to accept
some help.

It worked out for a little bit. I did well, I was going to
school. I was at CFS [Children and Family Services] then,
but I was staying there. I was doing everything I was supposed to do at that time for my PO, but then some things
happened and I took off. That was my way. It was the way
I had always been. It was just my way. Even today I wres-
tle with those feelings— the fight-or-flight instinct that I
have, that happens inside me when I'm pushed up against
a wall, or I get hurt. It goes off in me—do I fight or I
flight? And I'm pretty good at both, except for I work on
that today. It sounds like it's just all that—fight or flight—
but you know what's in between those two feelings? You
know what's raging in between them? Total fear. Fear,
crying, everything. Everything I don't want to deal with.
It's that raw instinct that's there at that time. When it's
there, I think, "Okay, I need to breathe, and then we can
talk about whatever is going on." I learned how to recognize that and do different things when I feel that way. But
when I was younger there was really nothing in between,
nothing else I could do but fight or leave.

That's part of why I didn't share a lot of information

with my counselors or my PO. I was scared. I had fears that they'd institutionalize me again. At that time, I wasn't giving information to people who could do that to me.

Rachel learned that she had more responses to her feelings than the fight-or-flight instinct that had held her hostage in her youth. Treatment helped her to be aware of her thoughts and their link to her feelings and, finally, to how they affected her behavior. She no longer had to run from those feelings or medicate them with drugs. She could see them now for what they were—a child's way of coping with sexual abuse that would otherwise have overwhelmed her. With that understanding and healing, she could expand her options for dealing with difficult emotions.

When I went to treatment, Tim was running and gunning. He was starting riots. He was living like he had no family—going out and doing things that I couldn't be around anymore. I had gone a few weeks in treatment, and I told him, "As much as I love you, either you're going to get clean and we're going to do this together, or I'm prepared to do this alone. It doesn't mean I don't love you. I just love myself and my kids more today." And then he went into treatment. And the stipulation with Child Welfare at that time was that we couldn't live together. So after he completed treatment, he could see me and I could see him, but only as long as we didn't have the kids. By then I had gotten the kids back into my physical custody. He could have the kids without me there, and I could have the kids without him there, but they didn't want the kids to see us together because of all the domes-

tic violence. So we had a really rough time. We were
fighting a lot. I was jealous because I had three kids who
moved back in my care and I was alone, in a very small
town. He was out at a recovery house, and he was able to
go and hang out while I was stuck at home, once again,
with the kids.

He cheated on me, and we almost got a divorce. What
happened then was the weirdest thing. I saw the way
treatment changed me. Instead of using drugs to cope
with it all, I got really angry at myself. And it was at that
time that I decided what kind of woman I was going to
be. I was with someone who was relapsing and he was
cheating on me. And I said, "Check it out. I'm going back
to school, I'm going to be an awesome mom, I am going
to take care of myself and my kids now. You can be part
of this or you can get going. I don't need you anymore.
I'm not going to be all the ways we were together in the
past." I was done with it. And it was the first time that I
realized I didn't need a man in my life to take care of myself.

It was a different kind of power. I knew it—I said
it: I'm not going to be abused like this. I'm better than
this. Treatment helped me start that path of self-esteem,
the path to knowing that I deserve something better than
what I had been receiving in life. And if I wanted that
better life, that better treatment, I had to set up boundaries. Then I had to say, "The way you're talking to me is
not okay anymore. We don't do this. These are my goals.
You don't get to interfere with them. They're my dreams.
They're mine—these are mine. They're my personal
goals for once." It wasn't like the goals for my kids;
these were my personal goals. I started making healthy
friends that he wasn't friends with. We still have that: I

have my friends, he has his friends, and that's just the way it is.

About that time I started taking care of myself, some men in his life stepped up and said, "Either you're going to work with this program of recovery and you're going to do something different, or you can go somewhere else." He needed it to come to him like that. So I started with my counseling. I did some posttraumatic stress work, the stuff with my counselor. That helped a lot because something happens when you get older and you don't have drugs affecting your brain anymore. Those things start coming back really bad, and I didn't know how to cope with them. I knew I didn't want to use drugs. I was put on a lot of antidepressants, mood stabilizers. I'm not on those now.

We went through marriage counseling, we worked things out. In a way it's like all that had to happen. My husband is pretty chauvinistic. He's been working on it, but his view of women, because of the way he was brought up, is not very accurate, and I've not allowed that anymore. How could you let a man treat your two daughters like that? He always says, "Well, they're my girls." And I tell him, "I'm their mother." Also, I'm not very codependent anymore. I don't have to take care of him. I get to take care of myself.

The system needs some fixing. I think the system needs to be fixed before the kids get introduced to it, but how do you fix that? If we see repeat offenders, we need to really look at that. Maybe they need something more long term, more intense counseling, especially with young women. If you see them again and again, there's definitely a pattern to how they are coping with whatever happened to them. I think there needs to be more intensive counseling, not so much punishment. But there's a reason why these kids are acting on these behaviors, and I think if we can get to the root of that, that could change a lot.

I think the girls need more open groups—this is something that I know worked for me when I got into the program of recovery. These groups where women would come in and introduce themselves and they'd say, "I'm a recovering addict, too. I was involved with Child Welfare. I've been where you've been." There's a bond. So maybe if more people would set up groups, if more people would go and get their counseling degree or therapy degree and set up groups and say, "Hey, I'm a victim of abuse," or, "I'm a survivor of abuse. Here's a tiny bit of my story," I think that would help more people open up. Or when they sit down and say, "Hey, you know what, I've been a juvenile delinquent. Here are a few of the charges that I spent some time in detention or on probation for. I did some time." That can automatically create a bond.

As far as the shelter goes, that place they put me because my home wasn't safe, that shelter wasn't safe, either. I just don't think I should have been put there. I know they were trying to keep me safe and don't know how that could have been different, but it needed to be. It made things a lot worse. It's how I became a delinquent.

Here I was, right out of an abusive past, and they put me there, and the guilt comes. I felt like I was hurt, but I was the one taken out of my family, I was the one put in jail. I must have done something wrong. I think it would have been better if I was put into a safe house or maybe just a foster family.

The detention center was like a day camp compared to the shelter. Sure, at first I was actually terrified to go into detention, but once I got there, I got fed, I got books to read, I got to hang out with the juvenile delinquents. It was great. I got to go to school, and once in a while they showed movies. It was pretty cool. The people there weren't mean. And it was a lot better than where I was. At that time, when I got out of the shelter and was on the streets, I was at a crack shack. I was selling drugs. I was a teen selling drugs in a house that had no electricity. So, coming to detention, I got food and I got my headache cleared up. To me, it was a treatment, and no one really messed with me. I don't know why, maybe because I had my own cell. They gave them to kids who had been the victims of person-to-person crimes. So other kids there didn't mess around with us. It was pretty cool.

Today, after all this, this may be hard to believe, but I do believe in the system more than what I used to. I know that you guys have your rules and regulations and some of those I'll never agree with, but I do have more faith in it.

If I could speak to young women today, I would tell them there's something better, there's something better than what they're living. That there's always hope no matter what you have in your life. You have to have faith in something else.

You need a juvenile system. I've been involved with the adult system, but I have never been to jail. I have charges on me in the adult system, but I have no convictions. The juvenile system was enough for me. Okay, so I just didn't want to get caught when I got older, but I knew I didn't want to go to prison, I knew I wasn't going to do anything serious enough to do that because of the juvenile system. They gave us the statistics coming out the gate. If I kept on living the life I was living, this is what would happen to me. I believe in the juvenile system. I believe that there are a few kids, believe it or not, that get involved with this and never get in trouble again. But if you put them with a bunch of adults, those kids are going to be corrupted. Putting a sixteen-year-old with thirty-two-year-olds—we hear that happens in the prisons. Those aren't just stories, those things really do happen. We might as well be sentencing these kids to death. There has to be a juvenile system. I could not imagine a world without it. That would be awful, really. More mothers would be hiding out with their kids so they wouldn't get into trouble.

I believe more in the system today because I believe things have changed since I was in it. People are being held more accountable when a kid comes forward and says, "This is what happened, this is happening to me."

I don't trust all child welfare workers. Some of them I wish weren't in the job. I do have a short list of people I really don't want to work with. But I have a long list today, and I know that if I was to come to them and say, "Hey, this is what's going on with this client, can we get them help?" I know they would listen to me.

There were many people who did not listen to Rachel when she was a youth. She knew that child welfare workers who were quick to label her were not her allies. She could not tell them what they needed to know to help her. She did not see them as help. She saw them as part of the problem, and she feared they would send her away if she was truthful. She understands why she made those decisions, given her life as a youth and given the way some of them treated her. What she is less sure of, however, is how things might have been different had the legal system followed through with charging her stepfather for abuse and whether that would have changed her life and her relationship with her mother. She wonders if court action would have made the abuse more real for her mom and lessened her own abandonment issues given her mom's responses to her acting out. She sees the possibilities of how that might have changed things for the better while at the same time acknowledging that everything leading to this time has helped her to be the woman she is today.

[My mom] wouldn't have left me for him. I wouldn't have had all the abandonment stuff with me. But then, if all that happened, who knows if I would be here, where I am today. I don't know. I wonder if maybe there was some validation to what happened. Maybe I wouldn't have gotten mixed in drugs, maybe I wouldn't have gotten into more trouble, and I might have graduated high school. I don't know. I definitely wouldn't have met my husband. And I don't know if I would have such a passion for helping others as I do today. But my life didn't have that validation and now I have a great need to help other people live through the kinds of things I went through. We were screwed up as kids, but it doesn't mean we have to be screwed up as adults.

I went through treatment and today I do work for a twelve-step program, where I'm able to learn things like forgiveness and surrender and acceptance. And I can't make my mother see things the way I see them. She has her own life and all I can do today is be an example. Give her the compassion I wish she would have given me. And I also know that she has her own problems. I think that as a mother, her best defense is denial. She just has to think that it didn't happen.

I've tried to talk to her about it all and her role in it. I was about to do that a few times. I'd say, "You know,

Mom, I have some abandonment issues." And she'd say, "I
have abandonment issues with you, too." And I said, "Oh,
really? What are they? I'd like to know." And she told me
that they had to do with when I moved to my dad's. And
I'd think that this talk obviously isn't going to work. I
don't know if I can ever talk to her about it. She knows
what happened. She believes me now because my brother
came out and told her that it was true.

That was all in my past. Now Tim and me have been
together for ten years, and I have three beautiful children
that I raised very differently than I was raised—obviously.
I have a wonderful husband who's a great father. And we
both came from some hard-to-change histories. His story
is very different than mine. He grew up in crime that was
inherited. It was a legacy that he had to receive.

I searched for a life of crime because at that time it
was exciting and made me feel better than what I knew. I
was brought up differently. I searched for that lifestyle to
be accepted and to belong. It wasn't something that was
given to me.

Today we tell our kids, "You make this choice, this is
what's going to happen." We talk to them kind of like
what my lawyer, Bill, did for me. He said, "You make this
choice, this is what's going to happen. You make this
choice, this is what's going to happen. What do you want?
What do you want your consequences to be?" And we
give them choices. I have them very involved with sports
activities, and I show up. I'm present—that's something I
never had. I never had anybody show up. I did do sports
for a little bit. There was a time—a brief moment of
time—when I really tried to do something different. But
when no one would show up for me, I'd think, "Why do
this?" It wasn't for me. I wanted recognition from my
mother, so now I give that to my kids. I'm not horribly

strict with them. There are a few things you don't do. You don't kill anybody—seriously. I'm really big on not fighting. We don't use our fists. We don't put our hands on each other or other people. We talk our differences out. We don't take things that are not ours. We don't say words like *stupid*, *dummy*. We don't use put-downs with each other, or others.

I'm a pretty awesome parent. I'm not perfect, and I don't want to be perfect. I make a lot of mistakes, but you know what? I do yell at my kids once in a while, I get so frustrated. And then they look at me and I'm able to apologize and say, "I lost my temper. That wasn't cool. I apologize for that." I am an awesome mom. I'm not perfect, and I don't want to be, because if I was perfect, then I wouldn't be teachable.

Me, I'd like to get my bachelor's. I want to continue working with women. I know there are social services, but, looking forward, I think I want to get into something with government, where I can help make change. I want to help with changing the system because sometimes I think it's kind of backward.

Rachel's story challenges a long-held misconception that child abuse and delinquency are limited to those in lower-income brackets. Her story also illustrates what doesn't work in juvenile justice: her gateway to delinquency opened not because she was abused and began running away but because she, an abused low-risk girl, was placed in a living situation with high-risk, sophisticated criminal offenders.

Communities tend to provide services to the juvenile justice end, *or* the mental health end, *or* the child welfare end, but seldom to all three. As a result, youths are forced into a one-size-fits-all system that clearly does not fit all.

Chapter 4

Alan

Alan is currently incarcerated for a manslaughter he openly admits he committed. He represents the typical headline-grabbing offender who appalls everyone watching, who makes us wonder, "How did this happen, and how can we prevent it from happening again?" He is a reminder that even with all of the services available, even with all of the research pointing to what works, there are juveniles whose crimes catch up with them faster than the scientifically proven efforts can save them.

It would be easy to dismiss Alan as just another violent youth, a product of a violent society. It is only when you have the opportunity to examine the full scale of his life experiences that you can understand that Alan epitomizes the failure of the juvenile justice and child welfare systems.

Alan was born to a single mother in Washington, D.C. She had another child after Alan, a boy.

> The only thing that I remember about my mom is that she had a Bart Simpson tattoo on her ankle. She abandoned me and my brother in a crack house when I was

three years old. After that, I was placed in thirteen separate foster homes and two failed adoptions before I was
ten years old. Some of this was because of how I was acting up and arguing with my brother. At the age of ten, I
was separated from my brother and did not see him again
for over eleven years. The authorities told me that they
were breaking us up because we were fighting too much
and it made it too hard on the foster family. Without my
little brother around, I had a lot of time, because I wasn't
protecting him. So I started spending a lot of time with
the Gangster Disciples. The Gangster Disciples are much
more than a gang or criminal enterprise. There is much
more structure and more rules—unlike the Crips and the
Bloods, who are entirely criminal enterprises.

I had a place where I could go and people who would
take care of me. If I got picked on, the older gang members would stick up for me. No one else cared whether or
not I was getting beat up or fed. They also had expectations about how I was supposed to behave and what kind
of work I did. I know that sounds funny, that a gang would
care about how I behaved, but they didn't want somebody
acting stupid, getting busted by the cops, and calling a lot
of attention to them. They wanted me to be able to move
drugs from place to place without a lot of attention. I just
couldn't keep that life separate from where I was supposed to live, so I eventually was made by the courts to
live somewhere else.

Identified by the court system at the age of ten as "hard to
place," Alan was put on a bus and sent from Washington, D.C.,
to Hazelwood, Missouri, a town he had never seen, to live with
a person he had never met: his new adoptive father, a single

man who had already adopted another, older boy, this one also considered "troubled." Alan's adoptive father didn't impose any structure, rules, or expectations on Alan, and shortly after he arrived in Hazelwood, Alan was once again hanging out on the streets, the only lifestyle he understood.

Alan claims he walked in on his adoptive father looking at child pornography on the computer. He told a teacher at school and was subsequently removed from the house, only to be placed in a group home in St. Louis, Missouri, approximately one hour away. The charges were ultimately dismissed and Alan returned to Hazelwood, but he found that his father stopped enforcing any rules at all, and Alan's delinquency returned with a vengeance. He began stealing guns and storing them in the family backyard. He began drinking alcohol heavily. He was eventually arrested and referred to the juvenile division of the court. He had finally graduated from the child welfare system to the juvenile justice system.

> I don't know if my dad was scared of me then. We never talked about what I saw him do. He just let me do whatever I wanted. There is no way that he could not know what I was doing. There is no way that your kid can have over twenty guns stashed in your backyard and the parent isn't at least suspicious about it. I wasn't that clever of a criminal to hide this stuff very well. He just didn't care.

After numerous run-ins by Alan with local law enforcement and juvenile justice authorities, Alan's father decided to move the family to Hannibal, Missouri, a small city nestled on the Mississippi River, and a cross between Mark Twain's picturesque burg of Tom Sawyer and Huck Finn and an artsy vacation community. It has a population of just over 17,000 and is light-years away from Washington, D.C.

> I'll never forget how the cops treated me when I tried to enroll in school. They weren't going to let me in. I knew my rights and that they didn't have the right to keep me out of school, and I wasn't afraid to let them know it. When they finally figured out that I wasn't going to let them bully me out of my constitutional right to go to school, one cop told me that he was going to *let* me enroll, but if any big city crimes happen, he'll come after me. I tried for a while to make it work, but I still didn't have any rules at home, so my old habits took over and I started drinking again and the trouble started again. When I was little, I was smacked around and beat on all the time. Once I got bigger and I realized I was bigger, I decided that no one was going to hit me anymore. I was going to do the hitting.

Alan received twenty-three referrals for "minor in possession of alcohol," but he does not recall ever receiving any treatment. He was also arrested on several occasions for assault. He was put in the custody of the state and sent to a boot camp program in northern Missouri. Alan credits this program with helping him achieve maximum physical condition, but it did little in the way of addressing the driving forces behind his criminal behavior.

> I didn't mind the boot camp program. I know how to follow orders and I like to be physically active. It was too

easy. They told me when to get up, when to eat, when to go to bed, when to take a shower, and when I could use the bathroom. No one tried to hit me, I had plenty to eat, and they had some fun stuff to do, like working out. I think that they would consider me a model prisoner, but my whole life before that had been practicing for that.

After successfully completing the program, Alan returned to Hannibal on juvenile parole. He went back to school, found a girlfriend, participated in recreational boxing, and continued drinking, with little accountability demanded by his adoptive father. One weekend, while partying in a local park nearby, Alan stomped to death a middle-aged homeless man over a verbal dispute. Alan remembers little of the incident.

I was drunk, but I remember a couple of these dudes hassling me about this gold chain that I was wearing. They were saying stuff like I must be a girl if I'm wearing a necklace. I was actually walking away when the guy grabbed me on my shoulder. I just lost it. No one puts a hand on me. I just completely lost my mind and I knew that I had beat his ass, but I didn't think that I killed the guy. If he hadn't grabbed my shoulder, this wouldn't have happened. I've been hit too much, and no one touches me. I just blacked out. It wasn't until later that week that I heard that the guy was dead. I told someone at school that I had done it and they called the police, and I was arrested that day.

My attorney didn't try very hard. He gets six hundred bucks either way: win, lose, or draw. I gave him all of my background, everything that had happened to me, and I didn't hear any of it in court. I'm not saying that I didn't do anything wrong, but what about all the times I was hit, and worse? Shouldn't that count for something? Do you just throw me away? I know that I did something terribly wrong, but I'm going to be locked up for over half of my life.

He was convicted of first-degree manslaughter and is serving his sentence in the Missouri Department of Corrections. He has been there since 2005 and has sent his adoptive father countless cards and letters, including an apology note that he wrote for Father's Day, none of which have been answered.

What I did in a split second can change your life forever. I've spent my whole life searching for a family, and I went and took someone away from theirs. I caused the same pain that I've been running from all of my life.

The assistant district attorney who prosecuted Alan told us that she was struck by his eagerness to please, and later by his lack of hostility toward her as his prosecutor. Prior to our visit at the prison, our only contact with Alan had been through written correspondence. Alan's handwriting was that of an eighth or ninth grader, and his words indicated an almost childlike desire to please. When we finally met Alan in person, we were struck by the contradictions: the person we expected from the letters, the collegiate-looking young man standing before us, the streetwise gangster that he sounds like, and the monster portrayed in the media. He was polite and quiet, but expressed a desire to share his story, hoping that it might help someone else. The prosecutor's interaction with Alan, like ours, took place when he was sober. By his own account, he is a dramatically different person when he drinks.

> I have an allergy to alcohol. I break out in handcuffs every time I drink. I don't have a problem with drugs. It's alcohol that gets me into trouble. We sold drugs to punks. I wasn't going to be a slave to the needle, because somebody who's a slave to a needle can't be trusted.

This is an insight into how susceptible Alan was to influence, guidance, and direction. One has to wonder how different his life might have been had he been offered the structure, support, and encouragement of positive, caring adults. Alan describes his childhood as an unlucky break.

> My brother was lucky and got adopted by a good family. He is in the navy and is serving in Iraq. He found me about a year ago and came to visit me here. I just wasn't as lucky as him. I wish my adoptive dad would have cared more by setting limits and making me know that there were rules. If you don't set limits, then you don't care. I was just a check. But who knows, if he would have set rules I might have done exactly what I did. Someday I want to have a family. I will have rules and my kids will always know that I'm there and I care.
>
> I got my GED, but can't do anything else for the next ten years. You have to be within five years of release to get on any work crew because of escape concerns. You can't take college courses if you don't have a way to pay

for them, because you can't use tax dollars to pay for in-mates' college. If you don't have family on the outside to pay for it, you're screwed. I'm a smart kid who had a lot of opportunities to be stupid. So I spend my time working in the law library and reading everything I can get my hands on. I joined the multicultural group and am a Christian. I've got a lot of time to sit and think. The school resource officer in Hannibal was significant. He thought that I was trouble and I wanted to prove him wrong. Another one would be my mother. Because of who she was and what she did, I'm the way I am. I wrote her a letter telling her about me and that I understood why she did some of the things that she did, and that I forgave her. I asked her to forgive me, too. I never got the letter back. If I didn't send it to the right lady, I thought she would've wrote back and said, "Honey, I'm not your mom." I don't know why not hearing back from my mom surprised and hurt. If she would abandon me when I was three, why did I think that she wouldn't abandon me when I was twenty-one?

You have to think about others, you've got to have empathy for others, so that you don't do whatever you want to do without ever thinking about how it hurts other people. You have to put family as number one. Family is forever.

Alan will someday—when he's twenty-seven, or as old as thirty-seven—be released back into the county where his crime was committed, at which point he will be given twenty dollars, a bus ticket, and the property that he had on him when he came to prison: the clothes he was wearing when he was a seventeen-year-old boy.

How does our society produce a man like Alan? We have

mandatory reporting in schools, child welfare systems, juvenile counselors, drug and alcohol treatment programs, and foster homes, and still this young man was overlooked and thrown
away. Alan passed through thirteen foster homes and three
adoptions. The final adoption took him halfway across the
country to a state he had never seen, to live with a man he had
never met, a process that separated him from the brother he
loved, his only family. The only constants in Alan's life were
loneliness and abandonment.

Many children who start in the child welfare system mi-
grate to the juvenile justice system, carrying with them a
mountain of unresolved traumatic experiences. The notion
that a good home, without additional intensive treatment, will
overcome thirteen bad homes is wildly unrealistic. A lack of
proper assessment and appropriate treatment can result in a
case like Alan's. Boot camp made him physically stronger, but
not more insightful or skillful in addressing the root causes of
his criminal behavior. Alan recognizes that alcohol is a major
risk factor for him, but he has never received intensive alcohol
treatment.

None of this excuses his behavior. Alan's story isn't about
one moment in 2004, but about a collection of seemingly dispa-
rate moments from his entire life. There were numerous opportunities to intervene in ways that research has shown to be
effective, but instead he was moved through the system in a
predictable pattern, without serious attention paid to his particular needs. He also lacked any effective advocates on his be-
half. For most kids, one involved parent or mentor can make the
difference between a life of crime and one of responsibility.

Deep down I'm not that different than other people my
age. I want the same things that they want. I want a job I
can be proud of, a car, a home, and a wife and family. I

don't know that I can ever have those things, or that I would even know if I was on the right track to getting those things. I hear other people here talk about childhood memories like Christmas, birthdays, family dinners, and stuff like that. I never had that. The only routine that I've ever known has been when I've been locked up. There's something really screwed up about that and I know it. But I still want that perfect life. Even though I've done what I've done, I think that I should have a chance for something better.

Chapter 5

Stephanie

Stephanie is a guidance counselor at a moderately sized high school. She helps students plan for their futures after high school, whether that means college or vocational school. She also works with students who are at risk of dropping out of school. In short, she is a problem solver.

During the course of our interview with her, which took place in a local restaurant, we were regularly interrupted by former students or their parents stopping by to give her updates. Her first job out of college was as a juvenile probation officer, a position she held for over ten years. Very few people set out to become juvenile probation officers. Stephanie knew that she wanted to work with kids, to help them, but she wasn't sure what form that goal would take.

I saw an ad in the paper and thought, "Okay, it's working with kids, it has to have something to do with the court system—it'll be a combination of the two." I applied and got the job, and I was there ten and a half years. I loved it. I worked in the field for probably four and a half, five years, and then worked abuse/neglect cases for a couple years, and then took on the role of supervisor in the Callaway office for the remainder of my time.

I loved working with the kids and hopefully helping them make changes. I would have to say the abuse/neglect part was difficult. That was the hardest part. Not necessarily working with those kids—I liked working with those kids—but dealing with the parents and/or perpetrators of the abuse and neglect. That became a little too much at times, especially when I had my own kids. It was hard to see the effects of abuse on these innocent kids and not become enraged.

The line between child welfare cases and juvenile delinquency cases is a blurry one, and Stephanie saw this firsthand.

Many times they did cross over, but what causes it I don't know. I wish I had that answer because I think we saw kids from all walks of life come through the office. You saw middle class, you saw upper class. I would say the largest number did come from the lower socioeconomic class. We probably did see a higher number of referrals from kids that lived in what you would call the projects, but well-off kids were not immune to abuse and neglect. Juvenile referrals weren't defined by any certain money bracket, either. I didn't see that at all. If you saw a kid who was abused or neglected, you knew that there was a really good possibility that you would see them as a delinquent later on.

One fundamental question at the center of the ongoing discussion about juvenile justice is what makes some children delinquent. Is it nature or nurture? It is an age-old question. Stephanie isn't sure that she has a definitive answer, but her experience tells her that there are several factors.

I think some of it is curiosity and seeing if they can get away with it. With a shoplifting referral, for example, a lot of the time the kids had the money in their wallet to buy it, but wanted to see if they could get away with it. I think some of it goes back to drug abuse or at least experimentation. Those were a lot of the referrals. I still see that where I work now as a guidance counselor. I can pretty much guess who is involved with the juvenile office or who has been or who might be. Our at-risk group at the high school is most likely involved with the juvenile office or has been through child welfare services in some aspect. Many times it wasn't about their financial status but more about where their values were and whether or not their parents had an identified value system. If you perceive that everybody cheats or that everyone is corrupt, then you are more likely to participate in illegal behaviors. Also, if you were victimized as a child, you don't have a lot of empathy for others.

Identifying at-risk youth is not difficult, and staff in the school system know intuitively what many others have to be professionally trained to look for. If I see a student that walks in my office and has more than one F, is living on their own, or a kid walks in my office and says, "I'm pregnant," a multitude of things makes me less optimistic for that kid's future.

I know that oftentimes when we have an at-risk kid

that they have a parent that is struggling to keep a roof over their heads and food on the table. They don't have the time or the energy to make sure that their child is in an after-school program or involved in sports or other extracurricular activities that might prevent some criminal involvement. And although there are programs after school, there are not enough.

I think since I have the background of working with the juvenile court, I have a different perspective on it, but I think oftentimes teachers don't realize what kids deal with. I think that they think kids come to school and that's all they have to do. I don't think they have any idea that Johnny's getting possibly slapped around at home, or that Johnny's having to hold a part-time job to help pay the bills because Mom's the only one working, and Dad's on disability, or Dad's disappeared. I don't think they have any idea sometimes of what kids today are dealing with besides just coming to school. Or that if you say, "Hi, good morning," to them, and smile, that might be the only time anybody speaks to them the entire day.

As surprising as it may seem, Stephanie does not find her work as a high school guidance counselor to be significantly different from her work as a juvenile probation officer.

When I work with the at-risk kids, a lot of it is the same. The difference is that I work with a totally other group of kids that are college-bound. Not that some at-risk kids aren't, but I work with a larger group of kids who are taking their ACTs or SATs again, shooting for the highest-level scores, with the kids that are taking AP testing and making future plans. This includes that at-risk population. Oftentimes that at-risk group is looking to go straight into employment and not looking at that next step. If I get to work with them, hopefully it might open them up to looking at college. There are financial options out there to help you go on to school if that's what you want to do. A lot of at-risk kids, or the kids that we worked with through the juvenile court, didn't have a parent that went to college. Just because those kids are at risk doesn't mean that they couldn't be whatever they want to be. But it is also important that if they are employment-bound, we don't just write them off. They need to see what the work world looks like, because some of them haven't seen a responsible adult get up in the morning and go to work every day. Their worlds tend to be really small, and they don't know what's out there and available to them. They need to be told that they deserve a future, and that they deserve good things for their future.

It definitely takes a special person to be a juvenile probation officer. To do that job and do that job well, you have to love kids. You have to want to make a difference for them. The time commitment and the on-call hours would make it hard to go back and do that now, with a family. I don't know that I would be willing to do that myself right now, with the age that my kids are and with the things that I want to see for them. I think you need a single person that doesn't have a family of their own, someone that can put in the time that it really, truly requires. I know with the on-call hours and the lack of vacation time—and all those things that you had to be very careful about back when I worked in the office—there was no way it was going to get accomplished in forty hours; it just did not get done. They would need to have excellent people skills working with kids, getting them to open up. Writing skills are a huge necessity because of the reports to the court. I know we oftentimes had some people that were really good with kids, but they couldn't write their way out of a paper bag.

Writing skills and people skills are huge, organizational skills, dependability, responsibility—those are some things that are important. Some things can be taught, but some of the more intuitive stuff stands out to me. I can teach you policy and procedure, but I can't teach you how to be calm in a crisis.

I wore many different hats, especially when I worked with the Division of Family Services liaison position. You're a team member, but you're also the enforcer of what the court is saying. This team of professionals is also working with the juvenile office because youth in their care have been abused, neglected, and also committed delinquent acts. As part of this team, you're trying to enforce rules of probation, hold youth accountable, and give them the skills they need to be successful in the community. Many different hats were worn as a deputy juvenile officer. The integrity part of it and just the honesty and responsibility are critical. You had to know that you had people that you could trust and would be honest with the court and honest with the kids and the families, and have a backbone. You have to have the backbone to tell a parent, "I'm recommending your kids go to detention." You've got to have a backbone and be able to stand up and make recommendations, although they may not be easy ones.

About five years ago Stephanie left the juvenile court system for the public school system. Her position as a guidance counselor allows her to spend more time with her own children, but she misses the closely developed relationships that she made during her tenure as a deputy juvenile officer.

I did the job with kids, and I loved it, but when the opportunity that I would have summers off with my kids arose, I jumped at it, even though it was a pay cut and I had to go back and get my master's to do what I'm doing now. The juvenile office staff were a good group of people, and those were the kind of people that you had to have to run a good office. They were willing to put the time in that was required. And they did—we did, we were a good team. The law enforcement community or a parent knew that if they had a crisis at five till five, we wouldn't tell them to call back in the morning. It was tough to leave.

My most memorable moment, of course, was my very first case. I believed that I could completely transform every delinquent kid into a model citizen. I remember how I needed to prove myself, too. This first kid, Jimmy, came from a lot of poverty and generations of criminality. His dad was in prison and his stepfather was headed there, too. Jimmy's mother treated Jimmy more like a confidant than a son. I worked harder than Jimmy and his mother did to change his situation. When he committed yet another stealing, I was devastated.

One memorable kid was Randy. We worked with him because he threw a water balloon into a window and it broke, and the neighbor was just a real butthead about it. It's something that the neighbors probably could have dealt with, but they called the police on him and he had to do community service work, and pay the restitution on the window. After he was released from supervision, his sister committed suicide when only her infant daughter and Randy were home. She'd hung herself. And he wouldn't let the police come in and take her body down. He wanted us there. Randy stayed with us that night until his parents got back. They were truckers, and we didn't want him or his little niece to go into foster care, so we stayed up all night. He wanted to be in a place where he wouldn't have to talk about it. I stayed in touch with his mom for a while; she and I stayed in touch for several years. He was in the military, and to my knowledge is still in the military. But he wouldn't let the police come in. He wanted us, and we talked to him, and I know we told him, "You've done all you can do; you need to let the police do their job."

The highway patrol called me one night and demanded that I come out to the accident scene. There had been a rollover, a drunk-driving accident. It was a juvenile driving the car, and he was under the influence. The only kid in the car that was sober and had no alcohol in his system was the one that was killed. I called my supervisor and she and I went to a nearby truck stop restaurant and wrote our paperwork as the sun came up, and had to call the judge to obtain an order for blood testing. Speaking of wearing another hat, we worked with the parents of the deceased boy through that process, and they were grateful for how we worked with them, which was pretty different compared to how they were treated by the DA's office. They don't prepare you in college for how to tell a parent that their only son is dead.

When I think about the core things that I tried to teach the kids, I tried to make them aware of the opportunities or the things that they could do to make changes, but ultimately they had to make the decision to make that change. A lot of times it was more about listening, knowing that they could come in and talk and share what was going on. I would interject and make suggestions, but ultimately I was letting them talk. After hearing suggestions, they had to make determinations about what to do. What's the best thing for them? Is it staying in high school? Is it going to the alternative school? Is it GED? I let them talk about those options, and then assisted them to get those things accomplished. I spent a lot of time helping kids make plans about the next steps in their lives, even if they were just baby steps. Sometimes it was helping them plan or anticipate how to deal with the worst-case scenarios. It's pretty unreasonable to believe that a kid is going to give up his delinquent peer group, especially if he lives in a small town with a total population of three hundred people. He's not going to be able to avoid those friends and some of them are probably family members. Instead of just saying, "Don't hang out with your friends," it was far more reasonable to work with them on how to avoid bad situations.

Employees of the juvenile justice system tend to be offender driven, often focusing attention on helping kids and families get the skills they need to prevent crime. In this way we hope to keep the community safe. The focus is clearly not on the individual needs of victims. Stephanie's primary contact with victims was a result of damage to their property.

I was in charge of the restitution account. These people knew that on a monthly basis they were going to be getting a payment, or a letter saying payment wasn't received and the offender will be headed back to court and wouldn't

be making restitution payments. I know it was probably
four or five years before I left that the court got a victim
advocate, and I think that was a huge plus for victims. Before that it was just one more component of the supervisor's job, which became mine: getting those restitution
payments. I think most victims were very appreciative
when they received payment or contact from us. And oftentimes I think they were shocked that they were being
reimbursed, getting paid for what damage had taken
place. I don't think they expected it to really happen. I
think they deserved more information and more contact
from us, and that need for contact led to what is now the
victim advocate, at least in the circuit where I worked. I
think communication about the court process, about
what's going to happen if they've incurred any ex-
penses. . . . the court has someone to gather all that information on the court process and communicate it to the
victims and keep them updated, keep them involved so
they feel like a part of it.

I think the most important thing is working with the
kids, and so I think we have to be offender focused. But
could we do more with victims through the justice system as a whole? Most definitely. It's not just juvenile justice. Yes, we could do more. But the number one priority
has to be the kids, has to be the offenders, in my mind.
Victims do deserve to be heard. However, it would be really hard to be working with a kid and then have to sit
there and listen to the victims bash the kid when you've
worked with him for six to eight months and you're privy
to information that you can't share with them that would
explain a lot of why that behavior occurred. As many hats
as the juvenile department staff have to wear, being an
advocate for the victim makes it even more complicated.

The more that you can have people specifically assigned to work with victims, the better.

Working and living in the same community can be especially difficult for those in the juvenile justice field.

It was a little strange, especially when I worked for the juvenile office. A kid would get referred and I'd see that I went to school with their parents. I went to school with some people that had babies very young, and those kids were being referred to the juvenile office or DFS. Those were unique situations and were sometimes difficult, but I work with those same people now, because their kids are in high school. When I worked for the juvenile office, I think knowing the community as well as I did was a huge asset. Having that connection to the community probably opened a lot more doors to me early on, where I would have probably had a more difficult time just being a deputy juvenile officer.

Observers often assert that delinquent youths today are more dangerous, more violent than they were in the past, and that this is a reflection of a more violent society in general.

I think society has changed, and I think things are definitely still changing. I personally don't think that kids have changed that much. I think kids—be it if you look in elementary schools, middle schools, or high schools—are different shapes and sizes, but they're all kids at heart. I truly believe that. They may be involved in different things, or more serious things, as they get older, but they're all kids. We do standardized testing, and when they test—you would think this would be so minuscule to them—before each testing day, we'll give each kid a note. They might get a pencil one day that says, "Do your best on the test!" They might get a Blow Pop [lollipop] one day: "Blow the top off the test!" Just things with neat slogans. And my first few years doing it, I thought it was kind of dumb, that they don't really care about that stuff. Then two years ago we ended up giving them ice cream one day—the last and final day, because it was over—with "Scream that it's over with, you get ice cream!" They thought we had forgotten about the notes, and several classrooms buzzed in to the office because the teachers said the kids weren't going to test until they got their treats. That might be a silly scenario, but the point is that they're kids. I think the way society is, our kids are handling things differently, such as anger, and maybe we're seeing more violence in how they're handling things, but I'm not so sure. My husband made the comment that he can remember a kid bringing a gun to school when he was in middle school, and they just told him to put it away and not bring it back. That was over twenty-five years ago. No one today would ever respond like that, even though the behavior is the same. I know that there has been a lot of violent episodes in schools, but it is still a very safe place.

Chapter 6

Roger

Roger is the product of a typical 1950s nuclear family, a family with a deep commitment to each other and to their Mormon faith. Devotion and responsibility are ideas that he takes very seriously, and it is little surprise to anyone who knows him that he's had one employer for the entirety of his adult life, the local police department.

He's never strayed far from home, and he's shouldered more than his share of community hardship. Like many Midwesterners, he is quiet and self-effacing. He is modest in his successes and acutely critical of what he views as his failures. He is fully aware that any feelings of disappointment he's had during his life were caused not by his shortcomings but, rather, by the overly ambitious expectations he placed on himself as he worked to give back to the community. He originally envisioned his career in law enforcement as one where he would work with troubled young people and help create future doctors and lawyers. Anything less represented failure to him.

I didn't realize how much I must have stood out at the department when I started. None of my peers were interested in working with teens. They didn't understand why I was, and truly, I'm not sure I understood all the reasons myself at that time. It was just something I'd always felt. I knew what I wanted to do. I wanted to work with kids—teens, and maybe their families. I never questioned it. Now, it's easier to see the connection between my family and what I wanted to give to kids in my community. I felt if they had the opportunity, the support, they would turn their lives around and go on to whatever they wanted to do—become doctors, lawyers, whatever they wanted. I thought that if I had even a small part in helping them, then my service here was well spent. It seemed important, and it still does, to share the guidance that was given to me to help others. I thought it would make the difference for them. The difference that happens when someone listens to them, holds them accountable, works with them to set goals in their lives, and find ways to make their goals a reality. Let them know they are cared about. Looking back at it all, I wondered if I hadn't missed something—that I could have done better at it all.

Upon joining the police department, Roger immediately began working with the highest-risk youths in his community. These were delinquent teens born from generations of criminal behavior, juveniles who were facing charges of assault, rape, robbery, and drug dealing. Even in the early days of his career, acting primarily on instinct, his approach to working with youths and families in the community was the essence of community-based policing, a tactic that gets police officers out of their cars and in the community, either on foot or on bicycles. They spend more time talking to citizens in their natural environments: parks, schools, and other gathering places. It's an idea that's been gaining in popularity in recent years, and is typically introduced to a police force with training programs and the development of new strategies. But when Roger started work over three decades ago, it simply seemed natural to him to go into neighborhoods to engage teenagers, rather than expect them to find him.

He developed a program in the elementary and middle schools that brought officers into the schools to give students the chance to get to know them, and vice versa. The police had offices at the schools and spent their time talking to kids on campus, listening to them. This kind of positive relationship building helped prevent kids from getting into more trouble.

It made sense to me to be in the schools. After all, that's where the kids were. If there's a problem in their lives, you're going to hear about it at school. You'll see it at school. And the influence of teachers and counselors there can make such a difference. So the idea of having a law enforcement officer there to talk to them seemed like the right person at the right place. We worked on setting up an officer at the middle school. I met with classes and gave them information about drugs and how to avoid them. The kids were more interested in what was in my car than some of the information I had for them, but I let that work for me. The parts of my job that interested them were a great way to establish a relationship with me. It helped them to see me as a person and someone they could trust. I did see the difference that made in the school environment. I remember before there was an office at the school, we would get a call at the department about a fight occurring at school. By the time we got there, a lot of damage had been done. Kids, and sometimes staff, had been hurt. Other kids got caught up in the fight and sometimes pulled into it. There were the longer-term effects of retaliation. But when I was stationed on campus, and the kids got to know me, they would poke their head in my office and tell me there was going to be a fight. I got the opportunity to intervene before things got out of hand, to talk to the kids and facilitate their talking to each other.

There were a lot of kids and families I got to know when doing this job. One that comes to mind is Chad. He was a fourteen-year-old boy from a single-parent family. Chad first came to the attention of the police department through a 911 emergency call. When we arrived at a local hotel, we found Chad passed out on a bed with his clothes partially removed. The adult male who had made the call was evasive about how Chad had come to pass out but did say that alcohol was involved. Chad's blood alcohol content was found to be .36, which is over four times the legal limit and would be lethal for most people, much less someone who is under four eleven and eighty pounds.

Then I talked to Chad's mother and she told me that it was his first time drinking. I wondered how a kid that young could come so close to dying. What had happened and what would help to keep it from happening again? I gave him community service hours at the police department. I met with him, but mostly I wanted to make sure that he was meeting with his probation worker. I talked with him a bit myself. He had some challenges. Some things related to not having his biological dad in his life and about being raised in a biracial family. He still lives here. Chad had some other referrals but has managed to avoid serious trouble.

At the completion of the community service work, he thanked me for always being there for him. He said the experience in the police department had changed his view of authority and broadened what he thought he could accomplish. He also told me that he would stay in touch and stop by from time to time to keep [me] posted on his success. He did for a long while, but it's been some time since I've heard from him. You never know.

As we were talking to Roger, he received a voice mail message from another youth he had worked with. Right after our interview session, he played the recording for us. The young man apologized for not having called or stopped by in way too long, and explained that he had been working on a construction job in Saudi Arabia, and was now in California, continuing his education. He wanted Roger to know that he thought of him and his experience at the police department often, and that Roger had made a positive difference in his life. It was easy to see the impact Roger's involvement had had on this one young man.

Despite the obvious affirmation of the good that has come from his efforts, Roger openly questions whether his work with the highest-risk teens has really done any good, whether he's wasted his time and efforts. His ambitious desire to help troubled kids turn their lives around and become doctors or lawyers has often been met with the harsh reality that these kids come from generations of criminal behavior, circumstances that are difficult to overcome. He wonders if the brief time he was able to work with them was way too little too late to make any lasting change.

Funny that now that seems like such a big deal. I thought there would be more obvious markers in my community, that I'd see more kids get out of their family legacy of drugs and crimes. That didn't happen as much, and I

guess we'll never know how many didn't enter that lifestyle because of the prevention work we did in the schools.
It's easy to find the numbers of crimes juveniles commit;
it's harder to find those they didn't because there was a
turn in their path. But even with the harder at-risk families, something happened. They invited me into their
homes. We talked about the kids and what was happening
in their lives. You can imagine that didn't happen often
with the police in this part of town. I'm still in touch with
some of those families, and I probably learned more from
them than I offered. Too often we are quick to blame the
family and just see their dysfunction, especially if the
parents are using drugs. And it certainly causes problems
on many levels. But when we do that, when we just write
them off, we fail to see what's working in the home, the
love they have for each other. When you ask some of
those parents what they want for their kids, you know
what they say? They say they want them to do well in
school and hang out with better friends, the kind of
things we all would want. Their lives and ours are really
not that different. But their lives and ways of parenting
get in the way of getting to those things.

Roger set lofty goals for the kids he worked with, but never
failed to recognize the small accomplishments: completing
community service work, maintaining a C in a class, keeping a
commitment to stay in touch. Part of this is ignoring prejudi-
cial tendencies. Just because your dad and uncle have been in
trouble doesn't mean you have to be. In a community where
roots run very deep, judgments about neighbors and families
are generational. Roger knew that every family had its strengths
and was capable of supporting a child if given a little guidance
and faith.

Chapter 7

Michael

Michael is a sturdy, brown-haired, brown-eyed young man in his early twenties. He recently completed an apprenticeship at a local tattoo parlor in South Carolina and is now tattooing and piercing for a living. His shop is a hangout for teens on the fringe of society. They frequently talk about weekends of heavy drinking, run-ins with addicts and thieves, and more-than-occasional fights over anything from unpaid debts to girlfriends to general discontent. Michael reigns as a sort of elder statesman with the pierced and tattooed crowd who frequents his shop.

I know where these kids have come from because I've been there myself. No one really wants them now that they aren't cute and cuddly and have opinions of their own. If your parents can't control you, they don't want you. I'm originally from Arizona. My parents were teenagers when I came along. My dad didn't want the responsibility, so he left my mom holding the bag. Here she was sixteen years old, unmarried, living with her parents, and expecting a baby. No job skills, no education, no money— nothing. Her parents treated her like shit because she embarrassed the family name. Apparently my grandfa- ther's boozing and drunk driving didn't shame the fam- ily. My mom dropped out of school, had me, and tried to figure how to get the hell out of her parents' home. She hooked up with an older guy who didn't seem to mind that I was part of the package—at first. Mom married the old stepfather and moved in with him. By that time, my grandparents were real attached to me because I was cute, cuddly, and controllable, so they wouldn't hand me over to my mom. They told the cops that she was an unfit mother. My mom didn't have the money to fight them, and I think that the stepfather was secretly glad that I wasn't there taking attention away from him. Mom vis- ited as much as she could, but that was rough, with my grandparents trying to screw it up. She then moved with the stepfather so he could get a better job, so I saw her even less. By the time I was six, my grandfather had a heart attack and died. By then I was still cute and cuddly, but not very controllable. The school was constantly call- ing my grandmother so that she could come and get me. They said that I was constantly doing anything just to get attention. I guess I've been a "bad kid" from the day I was born. Still am. My grandmother decided that she couldn't handle me without my grandfather, so she called my mom and told her to come and get me.

My mom came and got me and I moved with her and the stepfather to Oklahoma. I went from being just an at- tention-seeking kid to a very angry attention-seeking kid. I was pissed that I had to move, pissed that my grand- father had died, pissed that my grandmother threw me away, and really, really pissed that the stepfather thought that he had some right to be in my life. My mom tried to smooth things over between us, but she didn't have a lot of credibility with me and no respect from the stepfather. She couldn't win. The stepfather blamed me for getting in the way of his life with my mother. If I got strep throat and they couldn't go out that night, he acted like I had gotten sick on purpose. One time I broke my arm and had to go to the emergency room. The stepfather swore to my mother that I did it because I knew that they had a little extra money in their checking account that month. Eventually, when I was around eight, the stepfather decided that he would beat a little sense into me. Perhaps the twelve-pack that he drank nonstop every day after work helped him develop his keen parenting skills. This was on a Friday night. I was so bruised up that my mom wouldn't let me go to school until Wednesday. She told the school that I had been a passenger in a car accident. Nobody asked me what happened. They knew. They just didn't care about one white-trash, pain-in-their-ass kid. They were probably glad it happened. "Good for them, the little shit deserved it. I wish we could kick his ass, too." My mom left the stepfather soon after that.

She had met my "new dad" at one of the fine drinking establishments that she went to. He wasn't bad like the stepfather. He liked to drink but he wasn't mean. He treated me like a drinking buddy, which I guess I was. I also was his chauffeur when he felt like he was too lit to drive himself. He always said that I wouldn't get in near as much trouble with juvie as he would in jail. I kind of liked him, but I knew that he and Mom wouldn't last. My mom didn't have money, education, and her looks were okay, but she was getting older. My mom was easy, let's face it. The only thing that she had, she gave away. She didn't want to be alone. I didn't count. She needed men in her life to make her feel that she was important and special. I used to not respect her for that, but I kind of understand it now. He got tired of hearing that Mom was whoring around behind his back, so he left. Mom went into full-out man-hunting gear. By then I turned sixteen. I think that I was a reminder that she wasn't young anymore, and might keep guys from hanging around. She told me that I needed to go out on my own. She told me that she became an adult at sixteen and she turned out fine, so she thought that it would be good for me because she thought that I was becoming too much of a "mama's boy." So I packed my backpack with my clothes, weed, and about forty-eight dollars that I had from birthday money that my grandma had sent me. Off I went.

My goal was to get to Florida. Nothing good ever came from where I was, and I wasn't going to waste any more of my time with the snow, ice, and city crap. I talked a friend, who was probably my age, into leaving with me. We planned that we would make it to Miami, where we would lie about our ages and get jobs as auto mechanics. We also knew that my money and what he brought along would not be enough to make it, so we started shoplifting for food and stealing money out of newspaper machines. As we traveled, we'd meet up with other kids and adults that seemed like us. My friend got picked up on a runaway warrant. Turns out some parents actually want their kids to stay at home. The cops said there was no warrant on me, and I lied and said that I had relatives in whatever stupid little town we were in, and they believed me or didn't want to work too hard to prove me wrong. They let me go. It didn't matter. I had a group of friends that for the most part traveled together. We got better at the shoplifting stuff and found that there wasn't enough money in paper machines to meet our cash needs. We started shoplifting bigger items and then having one of the girls that were in our group return them as a gift because she didn't have the receipt. Then she would get the cash and we could maybe rent a hotel room, buy some rock, order pizza, whatever. Some girls would get knocked up and then we were in the money for a while. She would get food stamps and vouchers from the Women, Infants, and Children Program. We could use them for food or sell them for weed or whatever. Some churches would help her and get her a place to live, or hotel vouchers, so she wouldn't be on the streets. That meant we all had a place to live for a while. That would all end when she tested positive for drugs and either got locked up in jail or placed in treatment. None of us used safe sex. I still don't. Life is about taking risks. We always had some in the group drop out, but always picked up others. There were always about eight of us traveling at one time. We wouldn't stay in one place for very long. Our goal was to get to Miami. Some states were tough to survive in because their laws about unsupervised kids sucked. Since we were a large group, most of the time cops just acted like they didn't see us because they didn't want to find foster homes for a big-ass group of dirty, druggy, mouthy teenagers. The only time we had cop problems was when one of us got caught shoplifting or holding drugs. Whoever got caught got left behind. It was an unspoken rule, but we all knew it. It didn't take long for us to figure out the special rules about shoplifting. Get a cart, act like you are really shopping, put items in your cart, and push it right out of the store. Don't stop when somebody says stop. Don't act like you hear them when they ask for your receipt, just keep going. Once you're out of the store, there was nothing they could do to you. If someone started to give us shit, we'd say that we weren't in the store but were getting ready to go in and return these items because they were gifts and we didn't want them. There was nothing they could do. We wouldn't be able to go back in the store again, but by that time we were ready to move on.

I don't want to talk about the bad times. I try to forget them. It didn't happen a lot, but it was bad when it did. You can tell from my size that I don't go hungry. That's because I know that going hungry sucks worse than anything that you can imagine. I won't even let a stray dog or cat walk past the shop without trying to give it something to eat. People do weird shit when they are really hungry.

I never made it to Miami. South Carolina was as far as I made it. I got picked up for felony stealing at a store and I got stuck in juvie. I thought that they would let me go when they saw that I didn't have a record, but they didn't. I think that it was probably because there was nobody they could turn me over to. My mom wouldn't return their calls, my grandmother was in a nursing home, I think, and I didn't really have anyone else. Finally, they decided to put me in a group home to prepare me for "independent living." What a fucking joke! I could write the fucking book on independent living, and they were putting me in a home with a sweet-faced twentysomething out of college who was going to save us poor, misunderstood delinquents. I played the game for a while but always had my eye on my goal. I took off about three times and was caught. The third time, instead of putting me back in the group home, they put me in a locked mental health center for "evaluation." I'm a lot of things, but I'm not a fucking loon. Half of the people in there were really crazy, playing with their shit and biting themselves. The other half was lying to get out of worse places, like lockup. After about thirty days of that place, the staff asked me if I wanted to try independent living group homes one more time. I don't think that they really "evaluated" me, but they wanted to teach me a lesson that they were in control, and that if I ran away again I could end up in a place like that—or worse—for a long, long time. Needless to say, I was happy to get out. The group home was not my idea of my home sweet home, but it could've been a lot worse. Nobody swore at me, beat me, or treated me badly. I didn't get close to [the staff], because the only reason they were there was because they needed the experience to graduate from college, and they needed the money to pay their bills. It wasn't because they loved kids. No one asked me what I wanted out of my life. They had a little list of accepted outcomes for a group home "graduate." GED, then vo-tech. It was easy to see that I was never going to be a brain surgeon, but I was a hell of lot more than they ever gave me credit for. I was there until I turned eighteen. I got my GED and the staff had helped me apply to a vo-tech school for auto mechanics. Once I turned eighteen and got out, I said, "Fuck that." I never went to the vo-tech school. Instead, I had made friends with a guy that ran a tattoo parlor while I was in the group home, and he let me hang and paid me to clean the shop. I really enjoyed the people who came there, the people who worked there, the hours the shop ran, basically everything about it. I became an apprentice and put in my hours. Eventually, I became a licensed tattoo artist. I make decent money but will make better money as my art develops and my client base expands. I also do body piercing. I have a girlfriend who is a college girl. She is going into business. We met when I tattooed a tramp stamp on her back. I gave her shit about it and she gave it right back to me. I guess it was love at first insult.

My mom came out to see me a couple times and will be back sometime this summer. We are more friends than mom and son. She told me that kids today are real pussies. I didn't say anything, but I don't really agree with her. I think that she was a real pussy relying on her parents when she got knocked up, getting any man she could so that she wouldn't have to be alone, and dumping me when she thought that I would interfere with her love life. We don't talk about that. We will never talk about that. Why bring up the past? She did what she did. I did what I did. Nothing can change that. We do love each other. I do know that if I have kids, I won't be the kind of parent that she was. My kid will always feel safe and feel wanted, even if he was an accident. I'll also make sure that he never, ever goes hungry. I don't care what I would have to do, who I would have to hurt, and what laws I would have to break. My kid won't ever go hungry.

What worked for me? Finding people who didn't judge me, who accepted me for what I am and what I am not. That didn't come from my family or the system. Now, I will say that the system probably saved my life— but not on purpose. It kept me from going to Miami, where I would have kept stealing and drugging. Eventually, I would have been sent to prison, or killed, or overdosed. The system interrupted that. Finding people like me out in the real world kept me from going back to that world after the system was through with me. If I could change anything about the system, I would have the people working in it actually experience what a homeless, unwanted kid experiences. Not actually take drugs, steal, or hook, but spend the night downtown trying to sleep when it's under thirty-two degrees and you've got a park bench or doorway and nothing else. I'd also tell them to try to go three days without eating or showering. I'd have them write down exactly how they feel about themselves and how they feel about the people they see walking past them who act like they don't exist. I would want them to try to understand how those kinds of things affect how you think and what kind of decisions you might make to survive. The problem with that is they would always know that they were in an experiment and that it will come to an end soon. Me and my friends thought it would never end. For some of them, I'm sure it hasn't. I also don't think that upper-class do-gooders make good staff. Not that they do bad work, I just don't think that they can ever relate to what people like me have gone through. They might have had problems with their parents, but not like me and my friends. One of my friends had been nicknamed "Abortion" by his stepfather. We all called him that. One day, he told me that he wasn't sure if he even knew what his real name was. I bet none of the staff at my group home had ever had anyone in their college classes named Abortion.

I don't feel sorry for myself. I've got a life, a home, a girl, and a future. I help a lot of kids around here. I'm still a bad kid. I'll always be a bad kid. I'm just not living a bad life.

Michael would not be considered a success by Roger's standards, but this former street kid has defied the odds to establish a stable home and become steadily employed. His desire for a family and companionship led him to join a group of teenagers who were like him: disposable. He was a low-risk kid who had slipped under the radar, only to resurface after developing obvious antisocial behaviors that he saw as necessary for his survival.

Michael is very clear in identifying why well-intentioned group home staff members don't always connect with teenagers. It is imperative that staff members have a good understanding of the differences between their own lives and those of the kids they work with. This shouldn't be mistaken for pity, but seen instead as an acknowledgment that these kids' lives have been challenging largely through no fault of their own. Kids such as Michael are actually offended by the sympathy expressed by social workers, and this almost always causes them to put up communication barriers, making progress extremely difficult.

Chapter 8

Chris

Chris speaks in an easygoing Southern drawl. He is a large teddy bear of a man with a quick wit and a quicker smile. He is hardly a prototypical prosecutor. But his appearance and manner belie an unshakable ethical code. Although he now prosecutes adults exclusively, he spent several years representing the juvenile court in the prosecution of minors, and over the years became a strong advocate for the rehabilitation of juvenile offenders. During his tenure with the juvenile court, Chris saw the best and the worst of the juvenile justice system.

> The environment that a person has been raised in is the primary driver of criminal behavior. It is not unusual for us to see third- or fourth-generation offenders. I might know the person from when they were a juvenile, and the other prosecutor will have prosecuted the parents or the grandparents. Some of the juvenile probation officers would have to tell me, when I got frustrated, that

I never see the difference that the system makes because I only see the ones that screw up and are back in court. The juvenile officers got to see the successes. It was easier for me to get down in the dumps about it. Those families had so many issues: education, poverty, substance abuse. Methamphetamines are the biggest problems. Kids were not just experimenting, but using hard narcotics. Kids in court were not only using, but dealing cocaine, meth, and heroin. Ten- and twelve-year-olds [doing so] were not that unusual at all. Not all of them were dependent, but all of them were users. The running joke at one time was if you had a white male from the upper-middle-class high school, it would be a marijuana charge—possession or dealing. It was unusual to see African American sex offenders. That was a white male juvenile offender crime.

My desire to help people came from my youth. My father was a recovered drug addict, and through my dad's treatment and what my family went through, I found that I could've been a screwed-up kid. I saw how easily kids in my situation could've taken the wrong path. Sometimes I took the wrong path but I didn't get caught. My father got help because some good people got involved at the right time. I started getting involved in recovery programs when I was fifteen or sixteen. At the age of eighteen I was serving on committees with adults. For a lot of these kids, that never happened. Nobody got involved in their lives.

What influenced me to look at prosecution and the law occurred when I was in college. I was a psychology major in college and I was debating whether or not to go to law school when my sixteen-year-old sister was killed by a guy playing with a handgun. He was twenty or twenty-one years old. She was in the wrong place at the wrong time and didn't really know the guy. He was showing off for some girls and shot her and killed her. I had never felt that helpless. We were waiting for the police to investigate, and there was a civil suit. I didn't know what was going on and what to expect. The kid took it to a jury trial and was convicted. I hadn't seen anything like that trial. TV shows about law had never impressed me, but what I saw in the courtroom impressed me. The district attorney impressed me, and I told myself that that is what I wanted to do. I can remember where I was when it happened. After the trial, I spoke with the assistant district attorney because she had a lot of contact with the family. The district attorney handled the case because the police screwed it up. Anyway, I told the assistant district attorney that I was going to go to law school. I got that pat on the head and the "That's nice." I was a sophomore in college, and three years later I was interning with her in the same office, working on cases. It was really cool. She did homicide cases exclusively, so that was a learning experience. When I moved to Missouri from Mississippi, it was hard to get into a district attorney's office if you didn't know someone. A law school professor had told me that I had a knack for prosecution, so I came to Missouri as a public defender and was in Boothill for about a year and a half. I then transferred to Sedalia. I didn't like it and I wrote to every prosecutor in the state of Missouri looking for another position. Kevin Crane, who is now a judge but at that time was the prosecutor in Boone County, interviewed me for an assistant position. It came down to me and one other guy. Kevin offered the job to the other candidate, but he called me and told me that he liked me a lot, but that this other guy had more experience.

He knew that the juvenile office was looking for an attorney, so he gave my name to the juvenile officer. I had defended minors in juvenile court, so I had that background, but not much more. From day one I loved it. Loved it. Massive caseloads. I told people it was triage; we managed the hemorrhaging. I didn't have the time to fix all of the gigantic, complex problems. Hopefully, the juvenile officer, who also had massive caseloads, could be called upon for that. I just had to stop the bleeding and keep 'em moving.

The juvenile adjudication and disposition process plays an important role in short-circuiting delinquency. There were kids for whom just coming to court had a lot of impact. I think it got their attention and became real, and they understood that there really were consequences for their behavior. More people were telling them what to do instead of just Mom, Dad, Grandma, and Grandpa. Then there were kids whose five older siblings had already been through court. Court meant nothing to them. For the most part, I don't think that kids take it as seriously if they don't go to court.

At some point some kids would need to be committed to state custody, either because of how bad their crime was or because they had just exhausted the resources that were available locally. I used to think that state commitment was pretty good leverage for a lot of kids. A lot of kids were very afraid to be committed. Sometimes it was just a lack of information, fear that they were going to be locked up in prison. It wasn't like that, but that fear certainly could be a motivator. Some of them were detained for a short period of time, and I'm sure it did affect them. Then you have the kids with the older siblings that went through the state system. Commitment for them was just a paper tiger. Frankly, the supervision level at the local level was more intense and the kids knew it. It was not unusual for kids who had the older, committed siblings to not fight a commitment recommendation—some even request it.

Some older, more sophisticated kids knew what to expect in court. They had gotten to a point where the adult system was less of a hassle than the expectations of the juvenile system: attend school, make good grades, abide by a curfew, complete community service, urinalysis, approved friends, etc.

The juvenile probation officers, in their hearts, really want the kid to succeed, and they know what the kid needs to do. They're constantly on them. They ride them hard to get them out of the lifestyle that they're living and into a more positive one. Adult probation officers are not nearly that hard. Their thinking is "Let's see if they get through this." To me, you're hoping that the kid might be the first person to escape the cycle of criminality and be the first productive member of their family. I don't know if you really expect that from an adult on probation. Prosecutors don't expect it.

Victims of juvenile crime rarely make the distinction between juvenile offenders and adult offenders. They just know that they've been victimized. Sometimes they look for more than the system can give them. Sometimes the victims don't act much different from the perpetrators. Sometimes they come from the same family, sometimes from the same neighborhood or community. Sometimes they can be as difficult to deal with and sometimes they are completely naïve to the system. They have no knowledge of it, no experience with it, and there is a wide range within that group of people. Some expectations are wildly out of perspective, others are grounded in reality. A lot of victims of crimes don't care who did it. For example, someone might expect a kid to go to prison at thirteen years old. A thirteen-year-old is not going to prison for stealing your car. As you talk to the victims, some will come around and understand it. Some wholeheartedly believe that the kid needs help and will be on the same page from the start. That was great when that happened.

Then you have the other end of the spectrum, where they want the kid to go to prison. They're angry and upset. I sympathize with them because when my family went through everything with the death of my sister, the police mishandled it. The guy who shot her had a lot of relatives in law enforcement. They did a lot of things that they shouldn't have done. Fortunately for my family, the district attorney said, "No, we aren't going to do it that way." So I appreciate what it's like being on the outside looking in. I know what it feels like when you're not getting a fair shake. I'd made sure that when I dealt with someone, we weren't doing something because Johnny's brother was so and so. We're doing this because this is what Johnny needs and what is in his best interests. I think that victims of adult crime are pretty much the same way. Some of them have expectations that are wholly unrealistic, and some of them are uninvolved. I believe in the mission of the juvenile probation officer. I really believe that the juvenile officer can have a real impact on most of the kids. The expectations are real, achievable, and, if you did it right, you can see the results.

When I started, kids who had court-appointed attorneys sometimes didn't get much in the way of representation. Sometimes in a public defender's office, the newest member was assigned to juvenile cases. Sometimes you weren't given any instructions except "Go forth and litigate." You don't know anything about juvenile court. This happened to me and I used my mileage reimbursement money to pay for a continuing education class on juvenile justice. Now the policy has changed and every public defender completes a tour of duty with juvenile court. I think it got better when that happened. Defense attorneys do death penalty cases and turn around and represent juveniles charged with burglary and stealing. The level of expertise has changed pretty dramatically.

When you're an assistant prosecutor, everyone knows you. Everything you do outside of the courtroom is under scrutiny and reflects on your job. In this job, I am constantly aware of my values and that I am modeling those values for others. I'm really aware that things I say just in passing and things I do just in doing my job could have a tremendous impact on a lot of people. I don't know that the assistant district attorney that dealt with my sister's case truly appreciated that she had such a profound impact on me. We were at a point where we didn't really have any faith in the justice system. When she stepped up and said, basically, "This is a crime and we're going to prosecute, and I don't care who his uncle and his daddy are," it restored our faith. It was truly a ripple effect, especially when you think about what an impact she had on me to make me go to law school and to do the things I'm doing.

At one point I decided to go into private practice so that I could provide all of the material things that I thought my family should have. In private practice, it was commercial litigation. I was fighting about money every day. I was fighting with my clients. I was fighting with them over how fast I would get them their money, how

much I would charge them to get their money. I was fighting who I was suing over paying my clients' money,
whether they owed anything and whether or not there
was a breach of contract. I got to the point that I realized
that I didn't care enough about this. So I went back to the
juvenile department and handled delinquency and depen-
dency cases. The parallels between those types of cases
are significant. How are you going to teach a child empathy and respect for others when that has never been offered to him? It's one of those "Do as I say, not as has been
done to you" situations. There's a disconnect there. How
do you tell a kid not to use marijuana or to go to school
when the parent is stoned out of their mind, isn't holding
a job, and isn't upholding any of the parental obligations?
It used to blow my mind to see parents go out of their way
to thwart anything that the juvenile officer would do to
help their kid and then have the nerve to show up at court
and act surprised that their kid screwed up. They would
always blame the juvenile officer and never take responsibility for their kid. The juvenile officers had large caseloads and were triaging themselves. So many parents were
modeling how *not* to take responsibility to their kids. I'm
not faulting them for asking for a hearing, I'm not faulting them for not agreeing to a recommendation, but when
they constantly drill into the kid's head that they did
nothing wrong, that the system is out to get them, what
are their parents setting them up for in life? How *not* to
be successful, and how *not* take responsibility for your
own actions. Sex offenses were the most common for parents to refuse to allow their kids to take responsibility,
even where there was DNA evidence. Under pressure and
guidance from their parents, the kids would change their
story from "It never happened" to "It was consensual."

Too many parents try to be their kid's friend. There was one kid that I prosecuted for a sex offense. When the judge found him guilty, he let out a wail like I never heard before or since. He went to detention and when he came back to register as a sex offender, he came in to let me know about his change of address. He told me that he knew that he was supposed to stay away from his victim, but they attend the same school. He wanted me to know that he would keep his distance, and he referred to her as the victim of his crime. He had gotten the message, but not from his mother. She had been an enabler throughout.

In between college and law school, I worked at a psych hospital in the adolescent ward. I remember one boy in particular. Every day, like clockwork, he would go off and have to be physically restrained. Never failed, always on my shift. Now, this was a boy who had never had a father. He had a devoted mother and grandmother, but no male role model in his life. He also had some pretty significant mental health issues. One day I came on shift early and said to him, "Do I need to give you a hug today?" To my surprise the kid looked up and said, "Yes." I did a double-take and said, "You're kidding." He said no. I told him if he really wanted a hug, that we would work with staff to make sure that he was safe, and that no one would tease him or make things worse. I was sure that if I could give him a hug, he would stop throwing these fits and getting restrained. We worked with staff and he had a signal for when he wanted someone to hug him. His fits decreased significantly. Not completely, but quite a bit.

When I received notice that I had been accepted into law school and turned in my notice at the psych hospital, this kid was heartbroken. My last night there I sat beside his bed for the entire night holding his hand while he sobbed and sobbed. I just repeated over and over again, "It's going to be all right. Listen to your mother and grandmother. It's going to be all right." I've never heard how he was. In my heart he's all right, I have to believe that he's all right.

Chapter 9

Marcia

Marcia's office is a dimly lit, cramped space located in the bowels of the local sheriff's department, one of three windowless basement offices that eight people share. It is crammed with books, posters, and myriad items that one would collect over a career in juvenile justice, including an animated dancing turkey figurine that was a gift from the juvenile court judge. Marcia is a no-nonsense supervisor who works hard and has an expectation that those around her, including the youth under her watch, will do the same. The title of supervisor is misleading. It evokes the image of an administrator behind a desk pushing paper and attending meetings all day. But, like many juvenile workers, Marcia balances an actual caseload with her supervisory duties, and is raising a family as well.

I was born and raised in mid-Missouri, and have lived here for my entire life. My mom died when I was twelve years old, and it sort of fell on me to take over the household duties. I kind of took on the mother role and did "probation" work with my brothers. I'm just kidding, but they could be a handful. There were practical things that had to be done, like making sure they had clean clothes, got to school on time, got their homework done, did they pay for their school lunches—you know, like conditions of probation. Just stuff that had to be done. My father had to make a living. I did what needed to be done. After I finished high school, I got married, went to college, and started a family of my own. Originally I wanted to be a police officer who worked with youth. I was inspired by one of my college instructors, who had retired from that job. She made what she did as a school resource officer and truant officer sound exciting. She met with kids and families to work through problems to make the school a safer environment. This person talked about the nobleness of the work and self-satisfaction that she derived from helping kids break the cycle of their criminal behavior. She was so inspirational. I thought to myself, "This is what I want to do with my life." I knew that I wanted to work with people but I didn't know specifically what I wanted to do until I took her class. From then on, I wanted to be a police officer like her. What she did was really probation work. I never did become a police officer, but I did earn my master's degree in social work, and my dream changed. I have always felt strongly that people need to be held accountable for their actions, but in a way that helps them not repeat the past.

I wear a lot of hats as a supervisor. Some days I'm a court liaison, child welfare worker, probation officer, staff supervisor, technical consultant to the schools, public relations officer, and custodian. My husband complains that I seldom work just a forty-hour week, but I think that it's important that I'm available for my staff. Sometimes that means that I come in early and stay late. Because I'm a supervisor I'm required to be on call twenty-four hours a day, seven days a week, including weekends and holidays.

I don't think that I'm special. Just about everybody that I know that works in juvenile justice does what I do. It really is a team effort. The most critical parts of the team are the kids and families that we work with. Whatever progress is made and success we have is mainly because they decide that they want a different life for themselves. I just help them along the way and try to get them hooked up to the resources that they might need. I just wish that I could help all of the kids see success, but there doesn't seem to be enough time or enough resources for everyone.

I'm a practical person, so I look for practical outcomes: things that you can see, things that can be measured. I don't spend a lot of time around building self-esteem and talking about the past. Kids will start to feel better about themselves and get along better with their families as they start to experience success in school and stop committing crimes and getting into other trouble. I know that I have to walk the walk and talk the talk for kids and families. I can't say one thing to a family and then do another thing with my own. Maybe that's just because I live in a small community where everyone knows everyone.

My view of juvenile probation work is a balance between community safety, victims' rights, and helping youth get the skills they need to get back on track. Number one is community safety. It's frustrating for victims dealing with the juvenile justice system because they don't see what we're doing with kids and families. They think in terms of traditional punishment like they see on *Law & Order*. Trying to get them to see the big picture and understand that we are trying to work for permanent behavioral change so that others won't have to go through their experiences can be really difficult. A lot of victims want their "pound of flesh," and they see that as locking the kids up. It is often hard for the victim of a theft or burglary to understand that incarceration may not be the best response or the one in the best interest of the youth or community, even though the value of their property is substantial and their loss has a huge impact on their lives.

Most people don't know that locking someone up teaches lessons, but unfortunately the desired lessons are not always the ones that are learned. It's a tightrope act, the art of probation work: recognizing the impact on victims, addressing the criminal behavior, and understanding that rehabilitation will increase the likelihood that criminal behavior will not continue in the future. The stark reality is that there are never enough detention resources, so there is a constant sorting of who is the greatest risk to the community. The few precious detention bed spaces are utilized for the greatest-risk youth.

I take the responsibility of managing the juvenile office budget very seriously. These are my tax dollars, too, and I don't want to see them wasted. There is a lot of need and never enough services to go around, and a dollar wasted might mean that a kid won't get what he or she needs at a critical time. I have always considered it a privilege to work for the juvenile justice system, but it is also an awesome responsibility. Part of that responsibility is that we hold ourselves as accountable as we hold youths and families. If I go to a conference, I don't treat it like it's a vacation. I go to all of the sessions even if I don't think that they are applicable to what I do. You never know when you might learn something that you will need the next week. I also think that it is important that I let others in my community know what I do. First of all, I am proud of what I do. It's an honor to live and work in the community that I grew up in and am raising my own children in. But it is also important that I let others know what their tax dollars are doing. Juvenile justice is always looked at like it's less important than the adult criminal justice system, that we just slap hands instead of doing the "real" work. When I let people at the schools, the PTA, the city council meetings hear about what I do and give them the opportunity to ask me questions, it really opens up their thinking and suddenly they see the value of what I do. This job is about relationships. Juvenile justice gets a black eye most of the time because we don't talk about what we're doing, so people assume that we aren't doing anything, or are just locking kids up. I have to make sure that people know that the juvenile office is here and what we do is important.

A supervisor once asked me to think about and write down a specific accomplishment that I'd had with a current client. I think the goal of the assignment was to identify and build on strengths of youth on our caseloads. This seemed like one more piece of busy work added to an already overloaded schedule. Truly, a waste of time, a pointless assignment, but I did it. I picked a kid who had really struggled with substance abuse, parental abandonment, school failures, and probation violations. He had a really rocky road on probation but kept on. He never gave up. After I finished the assignment, I turned it in to my supervisor and then I made a copy and gave it to the young man that I had written about. I didn't think much about it, and years passed. I stopped into a Subway sandwich shop while on the road with one of my own children, and I saw this now older young adult working behind the counter waiting on me. He asked if I remembered him. Kids always recognize me, but after five years they have gone from age fifteen to twenty, from teenagers with peach fuzz to adults with beards. They are always hurt when we don't recognize them. We have gotten older but they have grown up. He told me who he was and then surprised me when he said, "Wait a minute, I want to show you something." He reached into his wallet and pulled out a wrinkled, tattered, torn piece of paper. It was the paper that I had given him years earlier. He said, "I still have it. I carry it with me everywhere I go. This was the first time anyone had ever said that I was successful. It made a difference. I want you to know it made a difference. I never forgot it. I never forgot it even when I screwed up. My mom never, ever said I was successful." Turns out the assignment wasn't such a waste of time after all. You can have forty-nine failures, and one success makes up for them all.

Chapter 10

Tyrone

In a hushed school auditorium, three hundred people sit in rapt attention listening to a thirtysomething man in a wheelchair as he begins to speak. He starts by asking the crowd, "What is the most important thing that you would need to build a model car?" Several answers ring through the room, "instructions" or "glue" being the most frequent answers. He disagrees with the responses, and explains: "The most important thing when building a model car is not the instructions or the glue. It's the picture on the front of the box. To know where you want to get to, you have to know what it's supposed to look like. It's a lot like working with at-risk kids. If you want them to try to have a better life, you have to show them what that would look like, because most of them don't have a clue."

Tyrone was a streetwise kid, but he was so ignorant of basic life skills that he turned down a college scholarship simply because he couldn't conceive of what it was, what it meant. His journey from juvenile delinquency to law school was ultimately successful, but it came at a terrible price.

Tyrone was born in 1970 to drug-addicted unwed teenage parents in Kansas City, Missouri. His parents were ill prepared to raise a child, and he was made a ward of the court when he was fifteen months old. When he was two years old, his grandmother intervened and raised him, along with twelve children of her own, in a Kansas City housing project. Not long after, Tyrone's younger brother joined the family, bringing the household number to fifteen.

Grandma had two jobs, so she wasn't home a lot. My aunts and uncles on my mother's side of the family raised me and they weren't really appropriate. I never really knew my dad's side of the family. They were into drugs and alcohol. They would get high and blow it in my face and give me beers. I never had new clothes. Grandma was old-school and made me wear everything twice. You get talked about at school, dressed in the same clothes from yesterday. She made me wear the same outfit twice, even though I tried to get her to change the rotation. And they were always a size too small or too big. We also had to make our own sporting goods—footballs made of paper and duct tape, for example. Baseball was a game played with rocks and sticks. And one meal a day was a success. I grew up really fast. I was the first grandchild. Whenever I did something wrong, they would tell me to stop, but they couldn't keep from laughing, so I got positive affirmation for my cussing and hitting people. They told me the story about how a billy goat would always butt you when you were bent over, and taught me the phrase "I'm going to kick your ass." When I was in preschool, getting ready to lay down on my towel, I saw my preschool teacher bent over and those two concepts came together in my mind. So I ran over and kicked her in her behind. Then I waited for her to laugh like my aunts and uncles always did. She didn't laugh, and I got expelled from preschool. I didn't know what I did wrong. At home it was cute. I also remember when I went to school I would tell the teachers that if they laid a hand on me, my aunts and uncles would be there to take care of it before the teacher could get to their car in the parking lot. My aunts and uncles would be foolish enough to do it, thinking that they were nobly taking care of and defending their nephew. I didn't realize that every time I did that at school or in the neighborhood, I was jeopardizing their freedom. What I saw as hitting someone was actually an assault.

Mr. Joyner was the nice old man in the neighborhood. We came and begged for food, and he would feed us. He taught me a lot of table manners, and when I would eat in his house I learned to keep my elbows off of the table and wash my hands before eating. That was the most painful part. It would seem like such a waste of time because I was really hungry and just wanted to eat. In my mind, I said to myself, "I don't know what all this nice stuff is, but I want this for my family." I wanted everything that Mr. Joyner had. I even wanted the color of my carpet to be the same color as his carpet. I wanted his environment. If you would ask Mr. Joyner for money, he'd never give you money, but he'd put you to work. He'd tell me to show up the next day and we'd clean out his work shed, weed his garden, or move some dirt and rocks. One day I wanted to work for a dollar, and he agreed. It was an all-day project, but I was having fun and didn't have a problem with it. He asked me if I wanted some ice cream when the ice-cream truck came by, and I agreed. We took a break and ate some ice cream together. The last half of the day wasn't nearly as much fun as the first half, and when we were through with work, I went to him expecting to get my dollar. He gave me seventy-five cents, and I stood there for a while thinking that he was going to go in the house and get me my quarter. Mr. Joyner then told me that he had taken the twenty-five-cent ice cream out of my pay, and I was mad. I felt so cheated. Later that night, I snuck back and broke some of his windows. Even while I was doing it, I felt really conflicted, because I really, really cared about Mr. Joyner. I mean, I would have killed somebody over Mr. Joyner. But at the same time, he did me wrong, and I was raised to think that you don't let anyone do you wrong. You fight. Mr. Joyner had no pass on this. So I broke his windows and I didn't know how to reconcile this relationship. I walked past his house when he was outside and he would make comments like, "You're going to pay for my windows because I'm going to sue your parents." I always stayed away, until one day he said, "If you want to pay for these windows, show up to work tomorrow at six A.M." I was there at five thirty, and I worked to pay off the windows. I don't know how long it took, but I remember how good it felt to right a wrong. The thing that Mr. Joyner knew intuitively was that if he was expecting an apology, he would have to wait until I was at least in my twenties, or maybe I never would. I was taught that saying that you were sorry was a sign of weakness, especially if you thought that somebody had taken advantage of you and would go out and tell everybody. But Mr. Joyner allowed me to say that I was genuinely sorry through my actions. I didn't learn how to really say that I was sorry until I was in my early twenties, but he helped me reconcile a relationship without saying that I was sorry. Mr. Joyner and I have been talking for over thirty years, and every significant thing that goes on in my life, I walk to the old neighborhood and I share it with him. To this day, Mr. Joyner still gives me a card and a five-dollar bill for any of my accomplishments. He's the closest thing to a father figure that I've ever had.

When I was seven my grandmother became ill and a social worker came and placed me in foster care. No matter how poor I was or how little I had, that was where my home was and where my love was. My world was totally turned upside down. Everything that I thought was right, the social worker thought was wrong. I was told so many things, like, "Tyrone, if your family loved you, you wouldn't be here." Back then, being a dark-skinned African American was not popular, and I was tall, dirty sometimes, had nappy hair, and was smelly at times. I never questioned my self-esteem, because nobody loved me like I did, and I never questioned my family's love, because I knew that they loved me. To deal with the pain, I took it out on others and started fighting and breaking things and running away. It didn't take me long to go through three foster homes. In those foster homes, I was abused physically and emotionally. I was placed in basements overnight—and not in the nice finished basements but the dark, wet, dank basements with no lights, cold, with cobwebs. I remember spending the nights just sitting on the top step just banging on the door.

I was then placed in residential treatment, which was better. It was more sterile, but it was clean, it had structure, had things to do like Foosball and Ping-Pong, and I got three meals a day and snacks. I was the only African American in the facility, and one thing that you don't do in my culture is talk about your family. In residential treatment, the way you get your privileges is to speak up in counseling. So in order to get my snacks and privileges, I started making stuff up about my family. I didn't share any information so that anyone could help me. I was embarrassed by so many things that my parents were doing, but I kept it inside so no one knew how to help me. People are going to try to help you whether you tell them all the details or not. In trying to help me, they really hurt me because they didn't have all of the information to make critical decisions about my life.

At that time, institutions regularly medicated kids whom they considered "out of control," and Tyrone was no exception. He was given Haldol and Thorazine, and soon changed from a bright, inquisitive boy to a lethargic zombie, a frightening shadow of the child he had been.

I went in weighing ninety-five pounds, and four months later weighed a hundred and thirty-five pounds. I went from being the most athletic to only being able to sit and drool. I was placed in padded rooms, state hospitals, straitjackets, tested for mental retardation. Some of the issues were cultural. Professionals spent so much time trying to find out what was wrong with me that they couldn't see what was going right. I never went to a facility with a fresh start, because my file got there before I did. I swore that I never would cry, but when you are all alone in your room, you can't help but have a tear trickle from your eye down the bridge of your nose. I wondered if I was ever going to amount to anything. I ended up going to over eight group homes and getting kicked out of every one of them.

My dad died when I was ten, and I didn't really know him, but I didn't tell anyone that he was murdered, because I didn't want anyone to think bad about my family. I just told them that he was on a business trip in California. I remember people telling me that I would end up dead or in jail before I was twenty-one, just like my dad.

One care worker brought Tyrone to his home for Christmas, and this was the first time he saw a middle-class suburban home. Tyrone was impressed with the cleanliness and sense of order, and the abundance of good food.

I remember that they gave me a tour of their home and then told me to make myself at home. And they meant it. They trusted me without knowing me. I think they knew that I wouldn't steal from someone who trusted me. This same worker later said something important to me when I was acting out. He said, "Tyrone, you need to know that I can't like you any more or less than I do right now, and I really like you because of who you are. That's not going to change." From that I learned that every day was a fresh start. Before that, I thought that it was all or nothing. If I didn't get all of the points or privileges, then my world was ruined. When you think like that, if you've got nothing to lose, you get out of control and have to be restrained. Just knowing that Tony liked me and that this wasn't going to change made me realize that I could start over after a setback.

Mr. Hill was my eighth-grade teacher, and he always challenged me. In special education, you've got a hodge-podge of different talents, disabilities, or disorders, and I

was in a class with people who were slobbering on themselves. I just didn't see myself as one of those people. I
didn't judge them; I just wanted to be mainstream as
much as possible. Mr. Hill, instead of looking at my history or behavior, recognized that I had talent. I remember one time I tried to embarrass him in front of the class,
and he said, "Tyrone, you don't even know where you are.
Go and sit down." I went off. I started saying, "I'm in
room twenty-three on the Alice Robinson Floor. Alice
Robinson lives in Tulsa, Oklahoma, and Oklahoma is in
the Midwest, and the Midwest is located in the United
States, and the United States is in North America, and
North America is in the world." As I was going on and
on, I was pacing, because I knew that I was going to get
expelled for being smart. But Mr. Hill clapped his hands
together twice and said to me, "Don't let anybody ever
tell you that you're not smart, or that you don't know
where you are." He didn't spend a lot of time on it; he
simply left me to process it. It really impacted me. After
that he challenged me more and more, and held me to
higher levels of expectation.

My behavior became more out of control, and I was
punished more harshly. I was eventually placed in the
largest secure facility in the state of Missouri. When I
was released I was six four and two hundred pounds. I was
good-looking, popular, and athletic, and I could play basketball really well. That's all anyone knew about me.
When I aged out of the system at seventeen, I was released to my aunt, who was drug-addicted. We had no
running water; the utilities were often off. When the
utilities were on, we would have to take a light bulb from
room to room to have light. We used a sock in the bath-
tub because we didn't have a stopper. No one knew that I

was going to the corner store to steal milk and cereal to survive. That's how I spent my senior year. My aunt would use the food stamps to buy drugs. I couldn't tell anyone. I didn't want to be removed from my home again, especially for something that I didn't do. If I was going to be removed from my home, it was going to be for something that I did. I learned how to look good on the outside and keep the pain on the inside. I was groomed well, I dressed well, I smelled good. Everyone wanted me to go with them and be with them. Finally, I was at the A table [in school]—where all the cool kids got to sit. I was there because of how I looked and because I played basketball really well. I learned that the A table wasn't that great. They weren't better people. This was the best year of my life. I had two weeks of school left and basketball season was over with. I got a scholarship offered to me. I didn't know what that meant. I never thought about going to college, no one in my family ever went to college, and my school counselors never talked with me about college. Why would you talk about college with somebody who went to special ed classes and rode the short bus to school? So I turned down full-ride scholarships to four-year colleges because I didn't know what a scholarship was and I was afraid to ask. Instead I decided to go into the army, because I was used to having someone telling me what to do, and when and how to do it. Another plus was that I would get paid. I was influenced to go into the army by two movies, *Stripes* and *An Officer and a Gentleman*. In both of those movies, the main characters were told that they would never make it and that they weren't officer material, but in the end they did make it and they got the girl. Another influence was the television show *Little House on the Prairie*. My grandmother would make me watch it. The father just had his wife and kids and little house, but that was all that they needed. I thought that if I could just get my own house, I will have made it.

Tyrone had every reason to believe that the hard times were behind him. Everything changed, however, on May 23, 1988. He was riding a city bus with some friends when he got into an argument with another teen. Tyrone challenged the other boy to get off at the next stop to fight. He expected a fistfight, nothing more. But the other teen pulled out a .357 Magnum. In Kansas City in the eighties, gun violence was unusual, and Tyrone was shocked by the mere sight of a gun. Three shots were fired in rapid succession. One hit Tyrone's hand, another struck his leg, and a third went through his neck, grazing his spinal cord and leaving him paralyzed from the chest down and with impaired mobility in his left hand. While recuperating in the hospital, he was filled with thoughts of revenge. Through a chance encounter, he met an aunt and uncle on his father's side of the family. They offered him a place to live while he continued with his rehabilitation, and this was where Tyrone first encountered religion. With Christianity he finally found a sense of himself, and of peace, and his hunger for revenge gave way to a hunger for a better life.

What am I going to do now? My life was a struggle even up to this point. How am I going to make something of myself from a wheelchair? All my family grew up on welfare. I knew that the state was going to give me a check and a place to live, probably in the projects, and some food. I thought to myself, "Before I settle for what I know, let me see what life has on the other side. Let me step outside of my comfort zone and see what life is like on the other side of the fence."

Equipped with a motorized wheelchair, Tyrone attended community college. The distance from his home to the campus was approximately two miles, and rain or shine, sleet or snow, he went. He had a vision of what he wanted from life even if he didn't know what all of the pieces were or how they fit together. After graduating from community college, he enrolled at the University of Missouri–Columbia, and it was toward the end of his time there that everything started to fall into place.

I had one class left, the summer practicum. Basically, I had to write a paper and make a visit to a business. I chose juvenile justice because I knew more about that than anything else. So I visited the facility that I had been in. While I was there, a kid asked me why I was there, and said that there were only two reasons anyone came to the facility: either to write a paper or to get a job. He wanted to know which one I was. I took some time to talk to this kid because I realized that during all my time in the facility I just wanted someone to listen to me. This changed my life.

Tyrone graduated with honors, earning a B.S. in sociology with a minor in psychology. He then applied and was accepted to the University of Missouri–Columbia School of Law, and received the CALI Excellence for the Future Award for his work when he graduated. Instead of practicing law, Tyrone and

Rene—his wife, whom he met in Bible study class as an under-
graduate—established Higher M-Pact, a nonprofit organiza-
tion that provides tutoring, job training, counseling, and
recreational activities to inner city youths in one of the most
violent housing projects in Kansas City.

I know that this will sound weird, but in many ways my
paralysis saved my life. Before that, I was floating through
the only kind of life I had ever known. I didn't have a lot
of direction or purpose. All I knew is that I wanted a better life than I had ever experienced, but I didn't know
what that would look like. I could've stayed floating, but
misery doesn't just love company, it loves pain. I didn't
want to be in misery forever.

There are only three ways to get ahead. You either
have to have something to begin with, know somebody,
or learn something. If you have something, then everyone wants to be with you so that they can share what you
have. The problem with that is that it's really easy to lose
what you have. If you know somebody, everyone wants to
be with you so that they can associate with the influential
or important person that you know. The problem with
that is that relationships can change, and that person can
easily drop out of your life, and you lose everyone else.
For me, the only real way to get ahead was to learn something. You never lose that knowledge, and you can sus-
tain yourself.

In my neighborhood, there were a couple of gentlemen that I had identified as "successful." They had the
nice homes and the neat and orderly lawns. I'll never forget the lawns. The grass was green and cut. The gardens
were well kept. I saw these gentlemen working their yards

and taking pride in it. I remember sneaking up and looking through their windows and just being amazed at how
clean and nice they kept their things. They wouldn't let
you walk on their lawns because they wanted to keep
their grass nice. I remember as a little, tiny kid thinking
that I wanted that life. To this day, I won't let people walk
across my lawn because I finally have that perfect lawn.

Once in a blue moon, nice people with soft voices and
lots of initials after their names would show up and talk
to me in the group homes. They were assessing and diag-
nosing, but they never knew me and really didn't seem to
know how to reach me. It was the people who were there
every day that made a difference to me. That's why, with
the Higher M-Pact program, I limit the number of kids
that I work with to no more than ten at a time. I am available to them twenty-four hours a day, seven days a week.
Anytime that they need me, I want to be there. They
come to my house, they know my wife. We celebrate their
birthdays and any other accomplishments together.

I don't believe that the kind of work that I do can be
done as part of the system. It's just too intimate. I'm trying to create a sense of family and community. That's
also why I can't expand or franchise the Higher M-Pact
model. You just can't expand and still manage to draw
kids closer to you.

What makes the Higher M-Pact program unique?
We're looking at delinquent kids and assessing them for
the same leadership qualities that are found in CEOs and
other successful business leaders. Sometimes these qualities are masked by their behavior and delinquency. This
assessment is a lot like a talent search. For example, kids
who are running drugs are the kingpins in their community. This is seen as entirely negative, but what I can see

with those kids is real leadership potential. Higher M-Pact deals with the high-risk youth no one else wants to deal with. These youth are involved in the juvenile justice system and delinquent activities, and society views them as a lost cause. Although these youth are difficult and challenging, they possess many of the characteristics that also make great leaders: strong-willed, influential, and charismatic. They are facing the toughest challenges imaginable, but have qualities that can be nurtured into positive leadership.

Part II

How to Fix the System: Assessment and Recommendations

Chapter 11

A Brief History of Juvenile Justice in the United States

How did we get here? How did we get to a system that both offers hope and threatens to make things worse? The notion of juvenile justice is relatively new in America, with the first juvenile court appearing in Cook County, Illinois, in 1899, but the roots date back to seventeenth-century Europe. The juvenile justice system is often viewed as a shrunken version of the adult system. In fact, almost from its inception, it has been guided by the fundamental belief that young people are more easily influenced and molded, that genuine reform is possible through support and education.

The goal and purpose of juvenile justice work is threefold. First, it serves to support law enforcement in providing a safe community. To this end, juvenile probation offers a sanctioned set of behavioral limits, and assists police forces with supervision support and a supplemental form of observation that contributes to community safety. Second, it helps victims and communities recover as quickly as possible from the damage caused by criminal behavior. It's easy to see the kind of repair that needs to be done when property is damaged or stolen, but it's much more difficult to help a victim of physical or sexual abuse recover quickly, if ever. Third, through individual professionals, juvenile justice work teaches the skills necessary for young people and their families to live productively. Everything juvenile justice professionals do serves one or more of these three goals, and each aspect is as important as the others.

When we examine the trends and changes that have taken place since 1899, one important observation is that attitudes and policies that predominate in one generation often give way to attitudes and policies that openly oppose them in the following generation, creating a pendulum effect. The centuries-old debate on treatment versus punishment comes to mind. At times, increased rates of incarceration and sanctions are favored; at other times, treatment, education, and support efforts are favored—often depending on the current political climate.

Changes to the system have often been the result of society-wide inklings as to what makes sense when dealing with children, rather than the result of analysis of empirical data. Only since around 1990 have we begun to examine scientifically what works effectively in treating youthful offenders. Without data collection and tracking systems, the effectiveness of the juvenile justice system has been, and will continue to be, a hit-or-miss, knee-jerk one based on political winds and pendulum swings in cultural beliefs.

We must examine the system and the decisions that have been made regarding it in terms of strategy and implementation, much in the same way a clockmaker looks at an antique watch: He observes the way it's moving, and based on those observations, he makes incremental changes, small adjustments that are reversible if necessary. Then he observes again, looking for effects from the changes he's made, and makes further adjustments as necessary. Juvenile justice strategy must be based on solid research, and changes must he implemented slowly and watched closely.

—The roots of the American juvenile justice system go as far back as the 1600s in France. At this time, the infant mortality rate was rather high, and small children became valuable for their economic contributions to families. There was no time for childhood. Children were considered adults, despite the fact that they were emotionally, morally, and educationally underdeveloped. Because of this, in the eyes of the court, there was no distinction between child and adult. Youthful offenders were treated as adult offenders, and punishments in France at this time were harsh, including capital punishment for more than two hundred different crimes.

During the 1700s, the French education and religious reform movement challenged the perception that children were merely miniature adults, and thus began a gradual shift in the beliefs about the treatment of children in matters of crime. European criminal justice was, of course, still based on the idea that punishment was a successful deterrent, and this presupposed the criminal's ability to reason and make sound decisions, many of which were made in stressful situations. So with the new understanding of the cognitive differences between adults and children, the punishments for youthful offenders became less severe.

The next major shift in thinking about juvenile delinquency occurred in the early 1800s and originated in New

York. Family depravity and lack of parental guidance were considered to be the roots of delinquent behavior among children. The lack of values, discipline, and respect for authority, it was believed, led directly to delinquency. Local agencies began removing children from such depraved environments, and took another step by separating these children from adults in order to prevent "contamination." Most were placed in reformatories, but some were sent to rural institutions to learn cottage industry skills. Both models emphasized education and religion as the path to appropriate behavior in the community.

Around 1825, a shoe cobbler by the name of John Augustus went to the local court with an idea. He proposed that the judge release a man imprisoned for public drunkenness based on a guarantee that the man would show up for all future hearings and stay out of trouble. Augustus would keep tabs on the man and report on his progress in rehabilitation. He was, essentially, the first probation officer. About twenty years later, Augustus approached the same court and offered to provide the same service for youthful offenders, bailing out young people between the ages of seven and nineteen. A devout Christian, he believed that he could do a better job instilling the values necessary for them to lead a morally correct life than the penal system ever could, and saw his actions as a moral duty.

The creation of that first juvenile court in Chicago in 1899 represents the official recognition that it's possible, through different types of intervention and rehabilitation, to help young offenders become productive members of the community. During the early years of the twentieth century, the "biological theory" had a strong influence on juvenile justice practices. This was a shift from the John Augustus theory based on morality to one based on medicine, which began with a physiological diagnosis and employed treatments that were seen as "cures." The biological school believed that, in most cases, certain people were predisposed toward criminal behavior by abnormal biological factors. These abnormalities could be identified by the comparison of what was normal with what was abnormal, based largely on certain physical characteristics, such as the shape of the head, the size of the hands, one's body type, and whether or not one had a twisted nose, wrinkled skin, large ears, or long arms. There was a belief also that chemical imbalances led to delinquency. One screening tool was the intelligence quotient (IQ) test, based on the notion that criminals were considered universally less intelligent. If a child had a low IQ score, he was considered a likely candidate for delinquency, and given "treatment." During this period, "delinquency screenings" were used to test, isolate, and treat anyone deemed delinquent. As imperfect as this approach was, it at least represented a shift away from punishment and toward treatment.

Most of the personality development theories that address delinquency are based on Sigmund Freud's theory of the conflict of personality and the concepts of the id, the ego, and the superego. It was Freud's belief that the internal turmoil and struggle between the id and the ego, balanced by the superego, led to healthy or unhealthy psychological development. Psychoanalytic theory places a great deal of emphasis on early childhood experiences, and a great deal of significance on the relationship between the child and the mother. Parents are therefore viewed as crucial factors in the development and formation of the child's personality. If a child is delinquent, it's a reflection of ineffective or inadequate parenting.

Freud's theories brought a shift in the approaches to reducing delinquency. Instead of focusing on the external characteristics and well-being of the individual, they began focusing on the internal struggle. Viewed as a psychological illness, delinquency, once it was discovered and pinpointed, could be addressed through treatment like any other medical ailment. Although still a flawed model, this more sophisticated approach did much to encourage and enhance the notion that young people could be helped through therapeutic treatment.

In the middle of the last century, focus turned to environmental factors. A child's living conditions were now scrutinized, with special attention paid to socioeconomic status—the prevailing notion being that people from impoverished settings were more likely to commit crimes. The family constellation was also a factor; children from single-parent families and large families were considered more likely to develop antisocial tendencies. Last, of course, a child's peer group was considered very important. Treatment during this period focused on improving children's environment with community-wide programs. Free-lunch programs emerged in the schools, job programs for teenagers were established, and recreational activities programs spread, the idea being that athletics encouraged pro-social interactions with peers.

The problem with all of these approaches was that each placed the responsibility for the behavior on some sort of genetic or environmental factor, and not on the child himself. The blame was seldom, if ever, assigned to the youth who'd committed the crime.

Some of the most significant changes to the juvenile justice system in America occurred in the 1960s, but they were the result not of any shifts in philosophy and/or treatment, but, instead, of a series of legal decisions. The U.S. system evolved from the English system of parens patriae, which was predicated on the fact that the king was all knowing. In the United States, this became the state or local government, of which the courts were an extension, and they became all knowing. The courts could and did make whatever decision they felt was best for each child. But this idea was challenged through a series of Supreme Court rulings.

In 1966, in *Kent v. the United States of America*, the court ruled that a juvenile court could not waive jurisdiction over a juvenile offender—and thereby send the juvenile to stand trial in the adult court—without a hearing. Also in 1966, in *Miranda v. Arizona*, the court ruled that statements made by a suspect while in police custody were admissible at trial only if the prosecution could prove that the suspect had been made aware of, and subsequently waived, the right to have an attorney present during the interrogation. This, of course, had a tremendous impact on suspects' rights, but was especially important for juvenile suspects, who might not always have the mental capacity to prevent self-incrimination. But the ruling that perhaps had the most significant impact on the juvenile justice system came down in 1967, in the case *In re Gault et al.*

In 1964, fifteen-year-old Gerald Francis Gault was taken into custody following an accusation made by a female neighbor that he had made a lewd prank phone call. His parents weren't notified, and his mother came home from work to find him missing. When she eventually tracked him down at a local children's detention home, she was informed that there would be a hearing the following day, but that she would not be permitted to take her son home. At the hearing, the judge postponed a final decision and ordered Gault to remain in custody, where he stayed for several more days, until he was released without explanation and told to return for another hearing less than a week later.

The witness—the neighbor who had made the accusation—wasn't present at that hearing, but the judge ruled nonetheless, stating that the witness's absence didn't matter. At the conclusion of the hearing, the judge ruled that Gault was delinquent and ordered him sent to a state industrial school for the remainder of his minority, which in Arizona at that time meant until he turned twenty-one; he would be released prior to that date only through due processes of the law. This amounted to an almost six-year sentence, much longer than the sentence an adult would have received for the same crime.

Gault's parents appealed the decision, and although the process was made convoluted by the fact that Arizona, at the time, didn't allow for appeals in juvenile court decisions, the case eventually made its way to the U.S. Supreme Court in 1965. The 8–1 decision overturned Gault's sentence, saying that it "was a clear violation of his 14th Amendment due process rights, since he had been denied the right to legal counsel, had not been formally notified of the charges against him, had not been informed of his right against self-incrimination [to remain silent], had no opportunity to confront his accusers and had been given no right to appeal his sentence to a higher court." In short, the decision granted juvenile defendants the same rights as adults during the adjudication process.

In 1974, the Juvenile Justice and Delinquency Prevention Act further changed the scope of juvenile justice. The act formally recognized that the adult corrections and juvenile justice systems were distinct and separate. The Department of Justice created a Division of Juvenile Justice charged with addressing juvenile justice specifically and exclusively. Each state, through this act, received a juvenile justice specialist charged with supporting and encouraging the professionalization of juvenile service delivery at the state and local levels. A centralized agency committed to enhancing training resources and intervention strategies, centered in Washington, D.C., was established to promote the development of national standards, and methods of working toward these standards, including the implementation of benchmarks to assess progress and evaluate effectiveness. One of the most important changes was a move away from institutionalization for what are known as status offenses (i.e., ones that would not be criminal offenses if they were committed by an adult). Examples include curfew violations, running away, and truancy. The new act, instead, required status offenders to receive services provided in the community. These services included counseling, mentoring, vocational development, and alternative education. Placement in shelter facilities and residential treatment homes was acceptable, so long as they weren't secure facilities.

The act disallowed the use of adult jails for the detention of youthful offenders, and specifically codified where, when, and for how long juveniles could be detained prior to contacting parents or legal guardians. The act further called for "sight and sound" separation between adults and juveniles (though this policy was exempted for juveniles waived to adult courts). The act also required states to assess and address the fact that a disproportionate number of minority juveniles were being incarcerated, and receiving longer sentences in addition. Overall, the Juvenile Justice and Delinquency Prevention Act of 1974 represented a shift, in matters of juvenile justice, away from state independence and toward a national agenda set forth by the federal government.

Despite the many significant changes that the adoption of this act ushered in, it has been up for elimination in Congress on many occasions. The single largest criticism of the act is that it allows states to forgo the evaluation requirements by giving up access to the training, technical assistance, and financial resources, and that this allows the treatment policies and practices to go unchanged while states hold on to archaic approaches.

As we moved into the last part of the twentieth century, America saw an increase in violent crime and serious criminal behavior by juveniles. The public attention that these crimes garnered often led to statutes that increased sentence times and challenged the definitions of *adult* and *juvenile* in the eyes of the court. These legislative decisions were the direct result of public outrage, and often coincided with funding cuts for juvenile services. Research into the effectiveness of punitive measures versus intervention was ignored, or not undertaken in the first place.

In the late 1980s, a new concept known as "balanced approach" was introduced and gradually codified into law. Balanced approach is an offense-specific response to juvenile crime. Rather than attempting to create perfect young offenders (the social work approach) or punish offenders into submission (the punishment approach), the balanced approach outlines three areas that need to be steadily addressed: community protection, accountability to victims, and competency development. Much like a milking stool, where all three legs are necessary to prevent the stool from tipping over, the balanced approach requires that each area be given proper attention. No one leg is more important than the others.

Community protection addresses the community's right to be safe. The most obvious solution would be incarceration; imprisoned individuals can't victimize the community. Other approaches include supervised probation, electronic monitoring, random call-in centers, and house arrest. If problems are arising from a lack of adequate supervision in the home, placement in a more structured environment might be more appropriate. The community could also increase law enforcement presence, patrols, neighborhood watch programs, and general supervision.

The second area of the balanced approach, accountability to victims, refers to the offender's responsibility to make amends to the community and to the victim. It is obviously much easier to repair the damage to property than to heal the damage a victim might experience from a physical or sexual assault, but offenders must be challenged to do so.

Competency development is the newest of the three concepts. It involves providing youths with pro-social skills, with *competency* referring not just to the skill itself, but also to the offender's ability to demonstrate that skill. The fundamental goal is to assist youths and their families in developing skills that will enable the youths to successfully maneuver their way out of the system and become productive members of society. An offense-specific approach means that each offender is assessed on the basis of the circumstances that contributed to the individual crime, and skills that specifically address those deficiencies will be developed. Basically, it's not a good idea to send a thief to anger management training unless he actually stole something out of anger. The skills developed might include: responsible decision-making strategies, social skills, or victim empathy.

The balanced approach was formulated to help meet the common goal of creating a better system, one that reduces juvenile recidivism, provides community safety, and emphasizes the need to include the community throughout the process. Many state legislatures have taken the step of putting the balanced approach theory into law, but, unfortunately, some of these policies have been offset by other legislative decisions. I the 1990s, many lawmakers and influential public figures that the system was inadequately addressing criminal beha

and that it was "soft on crime." These sentiments led to policies that reduced the minimum ages at which adolescents could
be charged with specific crimes and increased minimum sentences. The problem is that many of these sentiments, and the
subsequent decisions, were based on perceptions, and not on
empirical data.

Perhaps the biggest change in the juvenile system in the
last twenty years is that research is finally emerging on what is
and isn't working. After almost 150 years of operating on perceptions, from both ends of the spectrum, we are beginning to
collect data and make informed decisions on what the data indicate. There is a growing excitement that, with this research,
we can more effectively and efficiently address the issues surrounding juvenile crime by instituting proven programs. Finding a balance among the three aspects is crucial in this
process.

A Snapshot of the Juvenile Justice System Today

Juvenile justice systems across the country handle more than
1.6 million juvenile delinquency cases every year.* Each state
and locality has a different version of the basic organizational
model, and countless support organizations fall outside of this
formal structure. What follows is an illustration that explains
the fundamental components of the system and their relationships to one another.

---

*Juvenile Court Statistics 2003–2004, National Juvenile Court Data
hive, Department of Justice, Office of Juvenile Justice and Delin-
cy Prevention.

JUVENILE JUSTICE FLOW CHART

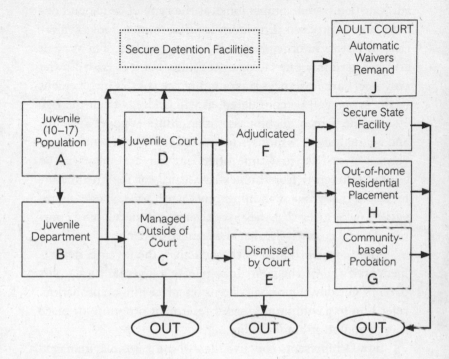

Box A represents the general juvenile population—children between the ages of ten and seventeen—in any given community. B represents the children who are referred to the juvenile justice system; this could be for criminal or non-criminal behavior. Criminal behavior includes anything considered a criminal offense in an adult court; non-criminal behavior, for the most part, includes activities considered illegal only for minors (e.g., running away, violating curfew, smoking cigarettes in some states, or truancy). In either situation, the juvenile justice system has to decide what should be done in response to the crime. This is one of the first areas where you'l see a difference between the adult and juvenile systems. The adult justice system simply looks at the type of crime and decides how to proceed. The juvenile justice system looks at a variety of factors in order to decide how to proceed. The type of crime is certainly one factor to consider, but it is far from the only one. Circumstances surrounding the youth's involvement in the crime will be considered, as will findings from the risk assessment, which encompasses the child's support systems, and an analysis of responses to any previous intervention services. Lower-risk, first-time offenders, for example, will be treated differently from higher-risk, third- or fourth-time offenders. Finally, age is an important factor; the juvenile justice system recognizes that these youths are still developing emotionally and cognitively, that they can still change.

After considering all of these factors, the juvenile department staff and/or the court may release a juvenile back to his parents' custody, put him in detention, place him on probation, refer him to a community-based treatment program, or place him in an out-of-home facility.

Box C represents the juveniles whose cases are managed outside of the jurisdiction of the court. They are supervised by informal probation staff. Informal probation is used for youths who commit less severe offenses—such as minor shoplifting, trespassing, or criminal mischief—and are less likely to re-offend. Informal probation allows the system to provide a response and a treatment program that won't occupy any more of the court's time. If informal probation is appropriate, the offender is provided with an action plan that specifies everything that must be done to satisfy the court, and by when. The typical time frame is between three and six months, and actions might include paying restitution to the victim, completing a designated number of hours of community service, attending n anger management class, completing a drug assessment, or getting specific types of psychological treatment. A probation worker monitors the offender's progress and assesses the effort being exhibited throughout. When the officer is satisfied, the case is closed. If another crime is committed, the officer can petition the court to have the child placed on formal probation.

Box D represents the juvenile offenders whom the court decides to formally monitor. This is typically initiated when a probation officer or district attorney petitions the court to adjudicate the offender. The court can either dismiss the case (Box E) or adjudicate.

At this point, in cases that are adjudicated (Box F), most offenders are placed on formal, community-based probation (Box G), meaning that the child lives at home or with a guardian, goes to school, works, and generally behaves like any other member of the community. Much as with informal probation cases, case plans are developed, specific actions and rules are identified, and a probation officer is assigned to monitor the child's progress. The distinction is that the officer, in these cases, represents the court, and the offender's progress reports are given to the court, which can alter the terms of the probation as it sees fit. Repeat offenses can lead to out-of-home placement (Box H). In some cases this can be a residential treatment facility for alcohol or other drug problems. These are typically not locked facilities, and are not to be confused with juvenile detention centers (Box I).

The last group of juvenile offenders, Box J, represents youths who are dealt with in the adult system. In the eyes of the law, they are no longer children.

Why do people work in juvenile justice? The reasons are as varied as the reasons children commit crimes. Some have passionate desire to help others, or a particular affinity for working with kids. Others have had some kind of traumatic event in their own lives, and enter the field in an attempt to fix that trauma by fixing troubled children facing similar circumstances. Still others use the juvenile justice system as a stepping stone to other, related careers in law enforcement or the practice of law.

It is not a job for the faint of heart. It is a job where you measure success in terms of small daily accomplishments rather than large victories. A lot of other careers offer greater financial rewards, but few offer a greater sense of personal satisfaction. There are, of course, moments of frustration and disappointment, but the best juvenile justice workers hope for the best and prepare for the worst, and spend little time lamenting past failures. The need is simply too great. On any given day, a juvenile probation officer can be expected to act as a legal assistant, counselor, public relations expert, investigator, program developer, disciplinarian, clerk, or mandated reporter. There is no such thing as a typical day; much of the work is driven by emergencies.

Why work in juvenile justice? Because despite all of this exhausting, stressful work, there is an incredible amount of satisfaction, and rewards that few people can fathom.

Chapter 12

What Doesn't Work

The insistence by professionals, and those familiar with the research, that evidence-based practices be used is warranted. There are corrections and treatment options that simply do not work, and in many instances they bring about more damage than good. This chapter looks at some of the more popular, and very often harmful, responses.

America has a romance with the idea of scaring youths out of delinquency, and this scaring can take many forms. A common tactic is a field trip to the state penitentiary, where youths meet adult inmates who intimidate them or make them feel ashamed or insignificant. The overall message is: "If you are feeling this way now, imagine it every day, in a small cell, with people like this." Sometimes these trips are captured in news pieces, in which the students cry or profess that they will never again commit a crime. And therefore the message to the viewers is that such a tactic works.

The problem with this seemingly quick fix is that it doesn't work. When you look at the research on hundreds of youths who go through one of these "scared straight" experiences, it shows that a significant number of them actually go on to commit more crimes. Why? First, let's look at whom this strategy is being used with. The scare approach does not work for high-risk offenders—those with multiple risk areas in their lives, those who have already committed crimes, etc.—because the shaming and intimidating involved in these interactions resemble the experiences that put them at higher risk in the first place, and so they consider the experience normal. Certainly, there are exceptions to this. You'll always be able to find a handful of high-risk youths who are moved by the experience. But overall, this scare tactic only sensationalizes a lifestyle they are already drawn to. It reinforces their decisions.

A second inefficient response is rooted in the belief in the power of education, or a classroom-style teaching approach, but information alone does not work. Youths must understand the relationship between their thoughts, feelings, and behavior, and then learn and, more important, practice new skills to replace the negative behaviors. Just providing information to youths does not create that necessary skill-building network. Programs that focus on delivering information with the intent to reduce crime among high-risk kids are a misuse of resources. That is not to say that information is useless. On the contrary, it is the starting place for youths to understand and become aware of the relationship between their actions and the impact those actions have on others, and the consequences of their actions to themselves. Information does not, however, on its own cause high-risk youths to make positive and difficult changes in their lives.

Open-ended counseling is also ineffective. This includes situations based on free-form, unstructured discussions. Again, in and of itself, this is not a bad thing, and it may even be beneficial for youths to get things off their chests. But it doesn't embody the principles of what works. It assumes that the therapeutic method that works with adults to help them through a crisis will also work to prevent a juvenile delinquent from continuing to commit criminal acts.

A very popular notion about juvenile justice is that self-esteem is the primary issue. The premise behind this approach is that the teens are shy or weak in some way relating to their self-image, and that if that characteristic could be diminished, they would become stronger and turn their backs on the influences of crime. There are two problems with this assumption. The first—remembering the risk areas (criminal beliefs, behaviors, attitudes, family problems, school issues, drug use, etc.)—is that self-esteem is not a risk area for crime. Think of all the shy people or those with low self-esteem who are not criminals. The second problem is that high-risk youths tend to have a very high regard for themselves. Almost all their decision making is based on what feels good for them. They think they deserve a better life, and whatever it takes to get there is almost inconsequential.

Another ineffective intervention similar to the scared-straight approach is to have the youths "exercise themselves out of delinquency." This is a kind of boot camp approach that suggests that rigorous exercise can somehow cause risk areas such as school problems and child abuse issues to be perspired right out of juvenile delinquents. It doesn't happen. True, it can be marginally helpful in some cases, but the overall data show no significant reduction in criminality for high-risk kids who undergo a program of this type compared with those who do not. Actually, what we create are juvenile offenders with high self-esteem who may be better equipped physically for future crime.

One of the most popular ineffective approaches is also the most controversial: moving youths to the adult system. Almo

every state has some version of this automatic waiver. It typically lists which types of crimes for a specific age group will
cause an automatic bypass of the juvenile justice system into
the adult court. These laws have been fueled by frustration,
fear, and the desire for quick fixes. The public officials who
support these policies are less concerned with changing behavior and more concerned with punishment. And indeed, criminals should receive consequences that are appropriately severe
for their crimes. But that alone will not decrease crime. Offenders who receive only punishment are much more likely to
commit crimes when they return to the community than those
who receive effective treatment as well. Moving a juvenile delinquent to the adult system will diminish his chances of receiving age-appropriate treatment responses.

The unfortunate aspect of this approach is that it is appeal-
ing in certain ways, especially because it locks up anyone who
may be a threat to the community. But several research studies
have found that it does not work. Except for the most heinous
offenders, most are released and return to their communities.
Studies that look at very similar groups of youths, some of
whom were referred to the juvenile justice system and others
who were sent to the adult system, found that youths who had
done time in the adult system committed more crimes upon
their release than those managed by the juvenile justice system. Why? Because they spent their formative years learning
about crime from adult inmates; because they did not receive
the treatment they needed to behave differently; and because
their experiences in the adult system left them angrier and
more damaged.

Some of these approaches have been documented to cause
harm. Others don't necessarily increase crime, but they don't
help reduce it, either, and so are taking time and resources
away from approaches that are effective.

Chapter 13

What Works

The narratives in this book represent the firsthand accounts of individuals who were or are directly involved in the juvenile justice system, a system that offers the potential for success, but also for disappointment. So what makes any one individual's experience different? What are the determining factors of victory? Of failure?

Many researchers have attempted to take apart individual stories of juvenile offenders to uncover the mysteries of preventing delinquency. And while there is much to be learned from these stories, it is misguided work, as it is driven by an effort to find that one crucial factor that forms a delinquent, or, at the other end of the spectrum, that transforms a delinquent into a productive citizen. This is clearly a fool's mission, but we persist in believing in these magic answers because we want teens to turn their lives around overnight. We want miracles.

The methods that work are centered on what are referred to as evidence-based practices. And before we walk through these practices and describe why they are effective, we want to give a brief background on the research studies that were used to identify them, because credibility in what works can be only as strong as the research behind it.

Let's look at a hypothetical program to examine the differences between evidence-based practices and unsupported practices. We'll call it the New Path Program, a residential lockup facility—meaning the residents live there full time—that serves older delinquent boys. The boys there have drug and alcohol problems, and each committed serious crimes before being placed in the facility. The goal of the program is to prevent these boys from committing more crimes by teaching them anger management skills and enhancing their employment opportunities. The program provides educational services, rigorous physical training, and anger management classes. About seventy boys between the ages of sixteen and eighteen pass through the program each year, and it costs the state $825,000 annually to fund it.

Observers regularly compare the number of crimes the boys committed before they entered the program with the number of crimes they committed after successfully completing the program. They find that the program reduces crime among graduates by 55 percent in the year following program completion. These observers cite an interview with one of the boys; he says he felt that the program allowed him to reflect on what he was doing with his life, and gave him the motivation to apologize to his victims, go back to high school with the intention to apply for college, and get a part-time job.

These findings are encouraging and compelling, because they are almost exactly what the public and juvenile justice employees want to see happen with delinquent youths: punishment, remorse, restitution, rehabilitation, and education. The assessment of the program is so encouraging that officials from other cities are soon visiting the facility in hopes of replicating the program in their own communities.

There is one problem, however: the assumption that the changes among the graduates occurred *because* of the treatment program. The observations were limited in their scope, and it was a grave mistake for observers to come to the conclusion they came to. As a result, continuing, expanding, and/or replicating the program may be a tremendous waste of funding and effort.

It's important to note that the research doesn't necessarily disprove the program's overall effectiveness. Discontinuing the program may keep other boys from getting effective service. The essential point is that the observations must be thorough. Careful, methodical research must be done before any conclusions or serious decisions are made. The most important question is: "What would have happened without the program?"

The first step is to establish a comparison group. It should include a random sample of boys, some who participated in the treatment program and some who received other types of punitive responses or treatment. The process used to select the comparison group is as important as having one in the first place. The comparison group should look as similar as possible to that comprising the boys in the intervention program, meaning that the boys in each should be similar in terms of the types of crimes they've committed; their age, race, and family background; their performance in school; and so on. If they are not as similar as possible, the findings will not be valid.

One hypothetical comparison group could be made up of boys who were given probation but who continue to live a home. They must report to their probation officers four tim a week. They are required to complete a certain numbe hours of community service, attend victim-offender medi if their victims agree to it, and receive intensive skills-building sessions at home, along with their family members. This treatment model costs $575,000 annually and serves eighty boys per year.

The observers would essentially be looking to determine if that 55 percent reduction in crimes among the New Path graduates was due to the program's efforts or if that same result could have occurred with other types of service, or no service at all. If the comparison group program—involving those on probation and living in the community—yielded better results while costing less per juvenile offender, doesn't that represent a better allocation of tax dollars? But if the comparison group program yielded less impressive results, then the New Path program has a stronger case for continuing to receive the public's funding.

This is the fundamental question, but there are many more that should be answered before either program is determined to be effective and/or cost-efficient. The point here is the idea of diligence. We must refrain from proclaiming that any one program is the best in terms of reducing delinquency until we're certain that it is based on sound research.

How "fit" was the research that led to the implementation of the evidence-based practices presented in this book? Instead of looking at a single program or even a handful of studies on multiple programs, the researchers looked at evaluations conducted on hundreds of treatment and corrections programs. They pored over the evaluations, their findings, and all of the data compiled, reviewing the fitness of each study as they went along. They essentially researched the research, declaring only ·tudies with strong designs as admissible. They were looking r two specific types of approaches: those that consistently *re-ed* juvenile crime, and those that consistently *increased* re-ism.

The results led to what are now called evidence-based practices, and are defined within these principles, which we address in the following chapters:

- risk (who)
- need (what)
- treatment (how)
- program integrity (how well)

In the end, the decades of research have validated what now seems like common sense: provide the right services to the right kid at the right time. This, of course, is no easy task. As they say, the devil is in the details. No one aspect is more important than any other, and each step in any treatment program must be carefully planned and reassessed throughout the life of the program.

Chapter 14

Risk (Who)

To determine if a juvenile is at low, medium, or high risk of re-offending, a well-developed risk assessment tool can be used. This is the first step in evidence-based practices, and is critical in terms of both making the most efficient use of the public's money and avoiding practices that may do more harm than good. In terms of cost-efficiency, risk assessment helps direct how to use funds to get the biggest return on the cost. The "cost" here is for the services developed, and the "return" is the resulting decrease in juvenile crime. Juvenile offenders who are at a low risk of re-offending typically need less intensive and less expensive services, while those at a higher risk need more concentrated responses.

Although this book focuses on youths who have progressed into the juvenile justice system, and on what works with that population, there are also many effective interventions for children of all ages that strive to prevent them from ever committing that first crime. These include programs that work effectively with high-risk families and their children of any age.

to reduce the likelihood that they participate in delinquent behavior later in life.

It is unfortunate that we as a national community get in our own way of providing those effective services. We have wasted much time and energy in this country by not recognizing the best ways to use our limited resources. We feel we must focus what we have on *either* early prevention for young kids *or* corrections lockup for high-risk offenders. Participants in that narrow argument contribute to the problem rather than the solution, which asserts that it is never too early or too late to work successfully with high-risk youths and families. There are cost-effective prevention and intervention strategies for this demographic at every stage of development, regardless of whether youths are in the general community, the juvenile justice system, or some other institutional setting. The important thing is to identify those at risk, determine the level of that risk, and provide a well-researched response that matches that risk level. We have more than enough resources to do this work; we just have to distribute them in a competent way. The reason it may seem that we do not have enough is that we often provide extensive services for low-risk youths and families, rather than triaging in order to benefit those most in need, or we spend funds on what doesn't work, even when we have the ability to use risk assessment tools to determine the most efficient courses of action.

Let's first look at what a typical risk assessment tool includes, and then go over why it is important to use one at all. Several tools around the nation have been researched and developed to identify a juvenile's risk level. Oregon uses a statewide tool that assesses risk level by studying criminal attitudes, beliefs, and behaviors; negative peer association; substance abuse; school issues; family management problems; and individual behavior. These are the key areas that have been shown to correlate to risk level.

First, criminal attitudes, beliefs, and behaviors can been seen in youths who have negative expressions about the law and conventional values, poor problem-solving abilities, and defeatist attitudes about their ability to be successful through conventional means (school, jobs, etc.), and who lack empathy and sensitivity toward others. These also tend to be pleasure-seeking youths who very often exhibit restless aggression. They can be egocentric, prone to taking risks, and have weak problem-solving skills. Chronic offenders typically start to show antisocial behavior at a very early age, and it can occur in a variety of settings.

Negative peer association is the second factor related to juvenile crime. In theory, those who spend their time with delinquent youths are more likely to follow in their footsteps. Peer relationships for high-risk boys are, for the most part, with other delinquent boys, whereas delinquent girls are more likely to associate with older men, many of whom are involved in criminal behavior. These girls are both criminals and victims, as the men introduce them to, or enhance their involvement with, drugs, alcohol, or felonious behavior. At one time, the system had a paternal attitude toward such girls. That is, runaway girls were "locked up" as much to protect them from these influences on the streets as to stop them from running away. Today, girls are much more involved in criminal behavior and violent acts, and that involvement is typically associated with their relationships to older males.

The third area of interest is alcohol and drug abuse, which is often associated with crime at any age. The myth is that drugs create criminal offenders, when, in reality, their use is another symptom of preexisting behavioral issues. Chronic juvenile offenders most often use drugs and alcohol to self-medicate; these substances numb the negative feelings they have not even begun to identify, feelings associated with abuse in their backgrounds, instances of domestic violence they've witnessed, grief and loss, or other traumatic events. The types of drugs most often used include marijuana, alcohol, cocaine, crack, methamphetamines, Ecstasy, and inhalants. Beyond the obvious psychological drawbacks of expression through substance abuse, drug use influences the decisions made in juveniles' daily lives. For example, delinquent youths may commit car theft, robbery, or other crimes while on drugs that they might not have committed while sober. The drug use therefore has negative impacts on their lives even if the crime is not necessarily a direct drug charge.

School performance is the fourth area studied to assess risk. Delinquent youths tend to have problems at school: chronic truancy, failing grades, expulsion, suspensions, getting high at school, aggressive behavior, etc. The classroom is one of the first gathering places outside the home where problematic behavior makes itself known. Teachers know this better than anyone. Many elementary school teachers report that they can tell who will eventually end up in the juvenile justice system by observing students as young as ten years old. And for the most part, their predictions are accurate. Youths with early antisocial behavior and educational problems are waving a red flag, indicating that without effective early intervention, there is an increased probability that they will experience significant delinquency problems in later years. It is estimated that 70 percent of juvenile offenders have problems in school. As with other risk areas, educational problems are not the cause of delinquency, but an indicator of its potential.

Family management problems have often been incorrectly targeted as the single greatest cause of delinquency. This might mean child abuse, domestic violence, inappropriate supervision, older family members in the adult criminal system, and drug abuse in the home. If any one of these was solely responsible for delinquent behavior, there would be many more children committing crimes than there actually are. That said, youths who grow up in these environments are indeed at greater risk of delinquency, making this the fifth area of interest when determining the level of that risk. An example of a common misconception within this conversation is that single parents or guardians are responsible for the delinquent tendencies of those in their care. However, anyone who grew up with a single parent himself, or who knows someone who did, knows that this is not the case. The quality of the parenting style is a much greater predictor than the number of parents, and that is an important distinction to make when evaluating family management.

Finally, the individual personal issues category refers to issues such as the age at which the first offense occurs. The earlier a child first becomes delinquent, the more likely it is that he or she will become a repeat offender.

The assessment tools that take all of these factors into account can be very helpful for anticipating future delinquency, and the research suggests that each and every juvenile justice system should be actively using these tools. However, these assessment tools must be thoroughly examined and routinely validated so they accurately predict the probability of future crimes. Assessments such as the Oregon Juvenile Crime Prevention Risk Assessment and the Youth Level of Service Inventory (Y-LSI) have been used, tested over time, and proven effective. Oregon's JCP tool, for example, has been validated by the Northwest Professional Consortium, and is now widely used. Typically, these tools are used during the intake process when youths first come to the juvenile department after arrest.

The Oregon tool's success is based on a scoring system that breaks delinquents into categories according to their level of risk. A youth at low risk of re-offending will score betwe zero and eight. A medium risk will score between nine and thirteen. And a high risk will score over fourteen. Statistically this tells us that if a youth scores fourteen or more on the tool, there is an 80 percent probability that he will re-offend in the next twelve months.

A low-risk youth may have been picked up on his first offense for a less serious crime, such as shoplifting or criminal mischief. But the level of offense is not a predictor of future indiscretions. The prevalence of risk factors is more of an indicator than the type of crime. And it is important to reiterate that these factors don't cause crime. They are indicators for youths in heightened jeopardy of delinquency. And the more applicable risk factors there are, the greater the likelihood that a youth will re-offend over the next year.

An example of a youth at low risk to re-offend is a boy arrested at age fourteen for stealing tools out of a neighbor's garage. He is doing well in school, doesn't have drug use issues beyond teen experimentation, his family doesn't have any significant family management problems, and his friends are relatively positive influences who have an awareness of right and wrong. Basically, he is a typical teenager who made a reactionary bad choice. He would score very low on the risk assessment tool, meaning he is at a very low risk to re-offend. Getting caught by the police, having his parents give appropriate disciplinary responses, and having the juvenile justice system involved at a minimal level are all effective responses for this indiscretion.

At the other end of the spectrum, the youth who is at a high risk to re-offend will have several risk factors prevalent in his life. He may also have been arrested for stealing the neighbor's tools out of the garage, but may have been involved in ther incidents of theft before his first arrest. He may also have ·umultuous family life, such as having an alcoholic father, and he may have started to drink and do drugs at an early age. He may also have been suspended from school for poor attendance or aggressive behavior, and may surround himself with peers who have also committed similar crimes. This youth may score seventeen on the risk tool. The impact of reaching this number correctly is significant. The goal is to identify who might be a repeat or chronic juvenile offender and to prevent that juvenile from continuing on that track. Effectively preventing chronic delinquency can translate into the prevention of thousands of crimes each year. How? Local, state, and national research has found that a small group of all juvenile offenders commit a majority of all juvenile crime. Roughly 7 percent of the general juvenile population is referred to the juvenile justice department for criminal behavior. Of all those referred, about 15 percent become chronic offenders, and they commit the great majority of juvenile crimes.

The payoff of assessing risk correctly cannot be overstated. Let's look more closely at that chronic group to understand just how significant it is. The following data, gathered from a local city in our home state of Oregon, make for an excellent example.

In one recent calendar year, 1,653 first-time juvenile offenders were referred to the court. A total of 878 (53 percent) of these offenders didn't commit another crime over the next 12 months, and 501 (30 percent) committed only 1 or 2 crimes, which accounted for 31 percent of the repeat offenses. Two hundred and seventy-four of those offenders (17 percent) committed at least 3 more crimes after the first, and accounted for an incredible 69 percent of repeat offenses, a tally of 1,470 documented crimes. If a jurisdiction can reduce the rate at which a juvenile becomes chronic, in theory it can prevent thousand of crimes. For example, if the above jurisdiction had a chror rate of 20 percent instead of 17 percent, it would have me more than 600 additional crimes in a single year. But if by using valid risk assessment tools it had been able to *reduce* the chronic group by 4 percentage points, the area would have had 600 fewer juvenile crimes in that year, which translates to a cost avoidance of over $2.5 million. The cost avoidance model is used in juvenile justice to financially quantify the impact of preventing crimes. The Lane County, Oregon, juvenile cost avoidance model, for example, looks at costs to victims, law enforcement, the courts, the juvenile justice system, and treatment, and calculates an average cost per juvenile criminal referral. Reducing those referrals yields an "avoidance" of that financial impact.

Research on the costs and benefits of delinquency reduction programs is currently very limited. Oregon is working on a cost/benefit formula for state-funded juvenile justice programs, but in the interim, Youth Services has developed very simplistic calculations in order to quantify the cost of juvenile crime and crime reduction efforts. According to their calculations, the cost of a single referral is $10,186. This figure is based on costs to victims, the juvenile justice system, law enforcement, and the court, including defense and prosecution. It is considered very conservative and is used consistently as a local cost proxy.

The reasons for using a validated risk tool should be obvious, and juvenile departments not moving in this direction are either naïvely dated in their approach or knowingly negligent with the public's funds. The tool allows justice officials to identify which juveniles are at low, medium, and high risk to reoffend, and therefore provides a map that shows who should receive less intensive responses and who should receive more concentrated responses.

Another reason to identify these groups is to make sure they are not "mixed together" in treatment facilities. Research over several decades has shown that putting lower-risk youths together with high-risk delinquents will actually make the former more likely to exhibit criminal tendencies. There is a contagion factor at work here: the lower-risk youths learn from their higher-risk peers how to be delinquent. This exposure can also sensationalize criminal lifestyles. Making sure that low-, medium-, and high-risk offenders receive appropriate responses in the appropriate environments can have a significant impact on our communities.

Here's our three-point challenge:

1. Identify youths in the general community who are most at risk of ever committing their first crime, and provide interventions that will prevent that from happening.

2. For youths who do commit that first crime, identify who is most likely to become chronic, and prevent that from happening.

3. For chronic juvenile offenders, provide effective interventions so these youths do not progress into the adult system.

Chapter 15

Need (What)

Determining who is at which risk level of re-offending is only the first step toward effective delinquency reduction practices. It will not, in and of itself, turn the tide on juvenile crime. Stopping there would be like having a tool that identified with extreme accuracy who will have a heart attack in the next year, and then not trying to do anything to prevent it.

The next step, based on the findings of the risk assessment tool, is to find out which risk areas are associated with the criminal behavior of a specific case, which we will refer to as the "need principle." In that sense, accurately using this method does more than produce a score. It lists which areas that are typically indicative of current or future delinquent behavior are active in a young person's life. Those identifiable areas are discussed in the previous chapter: criminal thinking, beliefs, and behaviors; negative peer association; substance abuse; school issues; family management problems; and individual behavior. Some of these factors can be altered and some can not. Obviously, something such as the age at first offense c not be changed, but most of the other factors are dynamic and can, with successful treatment, be improved. The goal is to provide services that systematically reduce the identified risk.

An important part of the need principle is understanding that no single factor causes delinquency. Rather, what is more important is the quantity and combination of the multiple facets of an individual's life; youths with multiple risk areas are at higher risk of becoming chronic offenders. Does that mean that all youths in this category become chronic? No. People will never be that predictable. About 10 percent of the time, a low-risk youth will become a chronic delinquent, and about 10 percent of the time, a high-risk youth will reform. But for the majority of the time—with 80 percent probability—a well-developed tool will be able to identify who is most likely to become chronic. The weakness in the tool lies more in getting accurate and thorough information from youths and their families than in the tool itself. In other words, not all the pertinent information is gathered at the intake assessment. While some may assume this is due to a lack of truth on the part of the interviewee, it is important to note that, surprisingly, most give correct information, even if they often do not disclose everything that may be applicable at the first intake interview. There are, however, interview techniques that lead to a greater trust between the youth, her family, and the interviewer.

One of the most effective of those techniques is called motivational interviewing. Staff members skilled in this technique are able to gather more accurate information and thereby improve the predictability of the tool. Motivational interviewing engages the family in the problem-solving process. Instead of conducting an interview in the character of a government worker, which may be perceived by the interviewees as distant and invasive, the interviewer must comprehend ways of interacting that will best resonate with most young people. For example, working from an understanding that the primary relationships for most people are with their families, interviewers must be able to find areas of strengths in the family's life. They then build on those strengths to address risk areas. For example, the interview may reveal that the mom is a hard worker and focus on that strength instead of condemning her for not being at home because she has two jobs. The interviewer takes the strength of her as a hard worker and applies it to strategies to increase supervision of the children at home.

This focus on what is working, rather than on what is to blame, helps engage families in the interview process. Despite dysfunction, most families have the same emotional goals. High-risk parents—parents who may have drinking problems, who may experience domestic violence, who threaten and even shame their kids as a reaction to problem behavior—have the same hopes for their children as well-functioning parents. Typically, they want them to do better in school, surround themselves with more appropriate peers, cultivate a respect for authority, and so on. The difference is that they don't have the same skills as every other parent to appropriately guide their children through the necessary changes, and the skills they do have can often worsen behavior rather than improve it. In many cases, they themselves are part of the problem and need to make personal changes to help their children. Motivational interviewing identifies the strengths in a family and engages the family to use those strengths to address areas of concern.

Unfortunately, even with the hundreds of studies that have isolated the factors associated with delinquency, practitioners are drawn to focusing on youth characteristics that they personally believe will make a difference—even if the resear does not support those beliefs. For example, many adults th that troubled youths just have poor self-esteem and that h dressing that issue they will produce better individua make more positive choices. Nothing could be further from fact. Juvenile offenders, for the most part, think very highly of themselves. Their egocentric view of themselves in the world puts them first and leaves little room for concern or empathy for others. The need principle argues for a focus on those factors that have been shown to influence criminal behavior directly and that can be changed effectively. Issues such as self-esteem levels, however, have not been shown to influence engagement in criminal behaviors.

As discussed in the previous chapter, chronic offenders typically exhibit criminal attitudes, beliefs, and behaviors that include antisocial tendencies in addition to the association with other delinquents or high-risk youths. The flip side of that is also true: chronic offenders have little involvement with prosocial activities. One of the claims of popular midnight basketball recreation programs is that they will keep troubled kids off the streets. There are three problems with this assumption. First, most juvenile crime occurs between 3:00 P.M. and 7:00 P.M. Second, while it provides social interaction, such a program doesn't address the areas that place youths at risk for delinquency. So you have juvenile offenders taking time to play basketball, but not getting the treatment they need to stop committing crimes. Third, there are successful proven programs that will make a difference in these youths' lives, but a game of basketball is not one of them, and so an opportunity is missed. This is not an argument to stop providing recreational services to youths and especially to high-risk youths. Recreation is a good thing, and is often part of effective programs. We need, however, to stop believing that, on its own, it is making a difference in delinquency. The directive of the need principle is utilizing the knowledge culled from risk assessment to develop programs that will be effective based on the areas strongly associated with delinquent behavior.

Chapter 16

Treatment (How)

Treatment has been referred to so often up to this point that it may carry a mystique all its own. But it shouldn't. There is nothing magical about effective intervention strategies. They are based on over forty years of evaluations of hundreds of programs. The research clearly points to what consistently works to reduce delinquency and what consistently does not work.

Before going into the details of what works and what does not, we need to settle an age-old argument about juvenile justice: Is it more effective to be "soft on crime," using treatment-oriented responses, or "hard on crime," using corrections responses? The answer is neither. It is more effective to be "smart on crime." And being smart includes a balance of corrections responses and treatment options. Corrections responses include probation, community service, restitution t victims, detention, residential facilities, long-term lock (sometimes referred to as training schools), electronic m toring, parole, intensive supervision, court involvement drug testing. How we handle offenders in each of these of the juvenile justice system determines how they go on to live in the community when the system has released them. So, to be effective, in order to provide a balanced intervention, treatment is necessary.

Since the evidence-based practices do not constitute a single program but, rather, the principles of effective interventions, they can be applied to both sides of the system. They can and should be part of the intake process, included in probation, used while offenders are in detention and while they are in community services, and even integrated into the juvenile court hearings. The research has shown that to be effective, treatment and corrections practices must do the following:

1. Match the dosage to the determined risk level.
2. Separate low-, medium-, and high-risk offenders into their respective groups.
3. Be community-based whenever possible.
4. Use a cognitive behavioral approach.
5. Provide gender-specific services.
6. Build on youth and family strengths.

Let's take a closer look at these steps.

First, the risk assessment is conducted to determine risk level and risk factors applicable to a specific case. The type of offense is not a predictor of future crimes, but certain types of offenses require specific responses. Based on risk level and type of risk areas, a case plan is developed that works to ensure community safety and provide treatment that addresses those risk reas.

Second, the categories produced by the first step must be ·rictly separated as possible, both physically and in terms of ·nse. Low-risk youths obviously tend to receive less-·ve responses. With this group there is a fine line between providing too small a response, such as a warning letter, and providing too much of a response, such as using interventions meant for higher-risk youths. The latter can actually increase their criminal behavior, while the former may not have enough of an effect. What this group requires are "diversion responses," which hold them accountable for their delinquent behavior and provide skills necessary for them to change that behavior. Appropriate responses for these youths may include having them complete community service hours, pay restitution to the victims of their crimes, or attend an anger management class with other low-risk offenders. In some areas, these youths receive services outside of the juvenile justice system, depending on their particular case. Often these cases will be referred to "youth courts," which are made up of community volunteers. Higher-risk offenders often have multiple risk factors, and therefore would not sufficiently benefit from these lighter practices. In addition to more typical correctional tactics, such as actual court appearances, the responses following release into the community must be more intensive. While education is universally accepted as the gateway out of poverty, it can just as easily be called the gateway out of delinquency. Nationally, over 75 percent of youths involved in the juvenile justice system self-report academic deficits, with 50 percent reporting suspension, expulsion, or truancy prior to their referral to the juvenile department. Enrollment in detention or court schools is one way to provide an environment for growth and reform while also continuing observation, a measure not needed for lower-risk candidates. Unfortunately, many alternative education programs are in peril due to budget cuts.

This book does not suggest that first-time or low-risk i nile offenders be referred to more severe parts of the ju justice system. It has long been known that more intens rections responses for low-risk offenders actually inc linquency. We also do not suggest that higher-risk juvenile offenders be referred to youth courts. There is no research on the efficacy of these programs for that population. What we strongly suggest is similar to national research: the key to effective delinquency reduction is to identify the correct response based on the juvenile's risk and need.

Responses that actively involve the community currently tend to apply only to low-risk youths, and those at higher risk require more severe responses applied in a professional capacity. Youth courts are one of three main community-based programs for primarily first-time juvenile offenders. Their function is to determine a fair and restorative consequence for these juveniles. They operate similarly to traditional courts, but instead of professional staff, volunteer community members serve in the roles of jurors, lawyers, and the judge. The jury can include, or be completely composed of, youths who have successfully completed the program, potentially putting offenders in front of a group of their peers. The court gathers information, asks questions, and then deliberates on a response.

While youth courts have grown in popularity and number—there are more than 1,700 in the nation—the number of rigorous evaluations of this diversion service is very limited. However, the studies that have been done show favorable responses. Research staff at the Lane County Department of Youth Services conducted an evaluation of local youth courts as part of their ongoing evaluation of all programs. The evaluation design included a comparison group of similar juvenile offenders who received a warning letter from Youth Services. Their findings indicate that youth court graduates went on to commit significantly fewer crimes than the group who only received warning letters. The difference is statistically significant with regard to long-term follow-up. The study found that at the two-year mark, the youth court was 10 percent more effective at reducing crime. The evaluation also included a cost/benefit overview. When looking at the probability of re-offending, the evaluation found that the efficacy of the court produced over $325,000 in cost savings.

Community accountability boards, another popular alternative to government intervention, also work with first-time offenders to negotiate an agreement of what the youth will do in response to their crime. This is referred to as a "disposition" in the juvenile justice system. Instead of a court setting, volunteer community members work with the offender to negotiate his sentence. The goal is to instill the reality that crime has an impact on the community and that its members should be involved in responding to it.

Victim-offender mediation is another community-based program based on the premise that the entire community ought to be involved in the criminal justice system, particularly the victim, who is often without a voice in more traditional proceedings. Often, depending on their situation, juveniles who would normally undergo an intake interview are diverted to victim-offender mediation upon referral to the system. This program requires voluntary participation by both the offender and the victim, and the offender must accept responsibility for his crime. If he does not, he is referred back to the judicial system.

During the session, two mediators facilitate a discussion between the victim and offender about what happened and what type of restitution is appropriate. The parties then draft an agreement on what the offender ought to do to compensate the victim and the community. This agreement can involve community service, restitution, a project, an apology, or an other task the parties deem appropriate. The offender m sign this contract detailing what she will do and when she complete the task. After the session, the juvenile is tracke her completion of the agreement recorded. If the offender agrees to mediate but the victim does not, the program proceeds similarly, but the agreement is drafted between the offender and the mediator. Research indicates that this program is effective at reducing recidivism.

These diversion programs provide responses that hold youths accountable, provide victim restitution, and limit the lower-risk offenders' experiences with the formal juvenile justice system and higher-risk offenders. The programs are supported by national research concerning the need for appropriate responses for juvenile offenders along the entire continuum of delinquent behavior. Findings of this nature have traditionally been met with calls for more severe responses for first-time offenders. This point of view is very common among audiences with limited exposure to research on effective delinquency interventions.

Treatment strategies for youths with multiple risk areas can occur in a variety of locations. For example, in a detention facility, during alcohol and other drug recovery treatment, and along with family counseling. These environments, or versions of them, can be effective on their own with low-risk offenders, but that design cannot be applied to high-risk offenders and still be as effective. Higher-risk offenders need more intensive treatment and corrections responses. Like their lower-risk peers, they may also complete community service, provide restitution to the victims of their crimes, or attend anger management classes, but they may also be placed in detention or longer-term lockup for juveniles at state facilities. During those placements, or in treatment settings, they should receive cognitive behavioral treatment.

Cognitive behavioral treatment sounds like something of the movie *A Clockwork Orange*. Here is the basis of the ment: thinking leads to feelings, which lead to behavior.

Cognitive behavioral treatment helps youths understand this relationship. They learn to identify the thoughts they have about themselves and their lives, and how those thoughts make them feel and, therefore, act. When a youth understands this pattern and the consequences it creates—in other words, when he learns to identify the thinking that triggers negative emotions—he becomes more open to making other choices about what he can do with those thoughts and feelings. Awareness, however, is not the secret to change. It is just a step toward it.

Think of it as teaching a kid how to ride a bike. You teach him the basics, watch him attempt to do it on his own, and look for areas that need to be improved upon. You don't assume he'll figure it out and correct himself. You show him what he is doing well and point out the problem areas. Then he practices the correct way until he's ready to have the training wheels removed.

A delinquent youth who understands the relationship between thoughts, feelings, and behaviors is like the kid who understands that he is throwing a ball incorrectly. He needs to see other options to use when those negative thoughts come up—new ways of thinking about himself and his life. He needs other options to manage his behavior and he needs to practice these things until they are part of his natural behavior.

So, cognitive behavioral treatment has a learning basis in which youths identify their cycle of thinking, feelings, and behavior and then find more appropriate options to practice and adopt. Most important, 80 percent of the treatment should involve practicing those new techniques in increasingly natural settings. This broadens their skill set so they leave the system with more positive skills than when they entered it.

———

People frequently ask if these principles apply equally to boys and girls, if they work for ethnic minorities, and if they are as effective in rural areas as in urban. The answer is yes. They have been validated by gender, race, and geography. When we think of juvenile delinquents, the image that normally comes to mind is of a teenage boy. It's true that, nationally, male youths are responsible for 65 percent of juvenile justice referrals. However, girls represent a significant 35 percent, which is a 6 percent increase from 2000. Of concern is not only that there are more girls committing crimes but that the rate at which they are committing them is also increasing. Girls in trouble have often been an afterthought in the juvenile justice system. The system is designed to deal almost exclusively with boys. Nationally, during the last decade, violent crimes among girls have increased at a faster rate than among boys. Gang involvement has also increased among girls. Girls are also becoming involved in the juvenile justice system at a younger age. Couple these disturbing trends with the woeful lack of placement resources for girls and you can easily see that the system is in crisis, and that the problem is too serious to ignore.

Although their offenses are typically less violent, girls who break the law are sometimes treated more harshly than boys in the same position. This is due in part to the lack of community-based treatment services available for girls. As a result, they are twice as likely to be detained, with detention lasting five times longer for them than for boys.

It must be understood that just as girls and boys develop in different ways physically and emotionally during adolescence, their pathways to delinquency are often gender specific. The problems faced by girls can be viewed as a part of a developmental continuum linking early problems, such as family dysfunction, abuse, loss of a primary caregiver, or other traumas, behavioral problems. Among female delinquents, an estimated 70 percent have a history of sexual abuse. Many girls report being intoxicated or under the influence of illegal substances while committing criminal acts, and female delinquents engage in sexual activity at an earlier age than non-offenders, putting them at higher risk of sexually transmitted diseases and unwanted pregnancy. The most significant risk factor relating to early onset of delinquency among girls is poor academic performance, and by the time they reach the system, many have already developed a negative attitude toward learning and their ability to master academic skills.

Over the last decade, an increasing number of juvenile justice agencies and systems have begun to look at the needs of girls separate from those of boys. Researchers have achieved an increased understanding of the developmental pathways that may be leading girls to delinquency, and practitioners have a better knowledge of what works in treating girls in the juvenile justice system. The combination of having more girls in the system with a better understanding of effective interventions for them challenges the system to work with girls differently.

Very few gender-specific model programs that could be replicated in other locales have been developed for services for girls within the juvenile justice system. The models that do exist build on the already impressive base of principles of evidence-based practice and include gender-specific drug and alcohol treatment, gender-specific respite care, and a gender-specific case management model to provide services to girls. Through this model, girls receive comprehensive assessment that, in addition to more typical risk and needs assessments, includes factors specific to girls. A rigorous evaluation model exists to determine overall program effectiveness and its impact on re-offending.

While these youths, male and female, are transient within a limited geographic range, the majority remain in essentially the same community into adulthood. This presents those communities with a significant challenge: to provide the services to assist the youths in becoming taxpayers instead of tax consumers (especially in terms of corrections costs). Providing education and employment opportunities to these youths offers hope that they will have the same opportunities and material possessions as their peers, or even the hope that their lives can be richer and better than their parents' lives. Providing these opportunities is no small task. These youths have difficulty managing their behaviors, and this cannot be underestimated. Additionally, the young people attending court schools often report feeling not wanted or welcome in their homes or alternative schools. With limited support staff, one of the real deficits in education is follow-up, support, and encouragement. Many youths who are referred to court schools benefit from the relationship and ongoing connection with a responsible and caring adult. Some have the skills to succeed in the academic work but need the problem-solving and relationship support to complete their academic programs. Only with individualized support can these youths be successful.

The partnership of education and juvenile justice provides the balance of intervention, accountability, and academic instruction necessary for productive results. The added components of workforce development and GED instruction provide options for those youths who are not likely candidates for traditional high school completion. These factors have been found to be surprisingly effective not only in improving the academic success of the attendees, but also in reducing crime. Many of the kids are very bright and skilled with their hands, or in ways that are difficult to assess in a traditional classroom. Faced with the prospect of supporting themselves with earnings from work in places such as fast food establishments for the rest of their lives, youths can often be filled with despair and a sense of hopelessness, which makes criminal activity more attractive to them. The development of marketable skills and meaningful work experiences can make an extraordinary difference in the lives of these youths. Court school and other juvenile justice/education partnership programs provide these very high-risk youths with real opportunities to better themselves, their families, and their communities.

Chapter 17

Program Integrity (How Well)

As jurisdictions incorporate these evidence-based practices into their programs, it's crucial to bear in mind that the practices are a comprehensive approach and not just singular, stand-alone items. Many jurisdictions are proud of the work they do for kids, and imagine that their work is unique, meaning that they need to change the nationally researched principles to fit the unique needs of kids in their community. Plainly put, altering the principles to fit a community doesn't work.

An example of this is mentoring programs, which are very popular in all types of communities. These programs can be effective for high-risk and delinquent youths. But it is not their name that makes them effective; it's their components, including highly trained staff, widespread mentor recruitment, good screening processes, excellent mentor training, administrative support, and ongoing supervision. Something may be called mentoring program, but without these components, the program will not be effective.

The integrity of evidence-based practices for add

juvenile delinquency is similarly important. The practices are effective only if conducted with the same components that have been proven to make them effective—components such as staff training on the principles, leadership from administration, thorough and ongoing review of the research, validated risk assessment tools, corrections and treatment responses that build on strengths to reduce risk areas, separation of youths with different levels of risk, intensity of treatment that matches risk level, and cognitive behavioral approaches in treatment.

There are assessments, such as the Correctional Program Checklist, that evaluate the extent to which a juvenile justice system is faithful to evidence-based principles. Programs and systems can use this national assessment tool to evaluate themselves against what is expected. The checklist is provided by officials trained in conducting the evaluation. It provides a score of how the program is doing in the areas of leadership, assessment, training, staff characteristics, cognitive behavioral approach, and evaluation. It also provides recommendations for modifications to better align a given program with the principles and the most effective interventions. The optimal use of the checklist is to encourage continuous improvement, not to punish service providers for areas of weakness. The result is that program and system accountability are equal to the accountability the system expects from the youths it serves.

Conclusion

O ne of the most stunning similarities among most of the juvenile offenders who shared their stories with us is the abuse and pain they suffered during childhood. They endured things that most people can't imagine surviving as adults. To make matters worse, the sex abuse, forced drug use, abandonment, and emotional battering happened at a time when they were unaware of the support they might seek to help them manage the impact of such trauma on their lives. The trauma happened when they were children and inherently vulnerable. Worst of all, the traumatic incidents were the results of actions carried out by the very people charged with protecting them: their parents and family members. When this happens, childhood dreams quickly turn into nightmares that can last a lifetime.

But as horrific as child abuse is, it is not the only thing ⸱ leads to juvenile delinquency. As we have seen, there is n⸱ gle cause of juvenile crime. If that were so, there wou⸱ greater number of juvenile delinquents in this cou⸱ stead, juvenile delinquency is increased when youths tiple risk areas—child abuse, drug use, school failure, family problems, intergenerational criminality, and negative peers—that coincide with a general lack of protective factors: positive adult role models, school attachment, pro-social activities, or a strong spiritual community.

In many of the stories in this book, risk areas accumulated faster than birthday candles, while protective factors were incredibly elusive. The question becomes: What made the difference between those who made it, such as Rachel, Michael, and Tyrone, and those who didn't, such as Alan? Those with success stories talked about adults who stepped in to become positive role models. The impact these adults made wasn't always immediate, but whatever they said *did* remain, and served to inspire change and dedication when the youths were finally ready to accept their role and make efforts to turn their lives around. Some of these adults were family members, but most of the juveniles were in harmful family situations, so help had to come from neighbors, teachers, or someone working in the juvenile justice system. Rachel's lawyer took the time to frankly explain her choices and the impact that each would have on her life, for example; and Chris was inspired by a district attorney who stood up for what she believed was right. The impact these people had on the lives of these troubled youths was remembered with the same clarity as the harm done to them—perhaps with more clarity—but it's not the adults who were the heroes of these stories. The narrators were subjected to terrible abuses, and it was those abuses—combined, of course, with the other ~sk areas—that led them toward criminal activity, behavior ~ was often just as unaccepted by the community as the ~ done to them. But when they were faced with crucial de- , they summoned the strength and resiliency to make ~cisions, to go through treatment, to get an education, ~luctive, to help others in situations similar to their own. Their adult role models offered guidance and reassurance, but it was the youths themselves who became the heroes of their own stories.

These influential adults knew intuitively what works to reduce juvenile crime and what doesn't, and they found ways to weave that insight into their efforts, whether through their individual work with teens or through programs they developed. Now we must move away from the current situation, in which some people understand what works while others don't. It's time to transform the secrets of the best practices into common knowledge. Juvenile justice workers must not only know what the approaches are, they must also practice them. Politicians must include them in their platforms, and victims must demand that offenders receive the best possible responses in order to prevent re-offenses. Our system must finally become part of the solution instead of part of the problem.

It is daunting to think that we must now sit down and design a strategy for this work. The debate on what works with juvenile offenders is an emotional argument. If you lean toward what helps youths, such as treatment programs, you're labeled "soft on crime." If you lean toward punishment that holds them accountable, you're "hard on crime." Fortunately, the research behind effective, cost-efficient strategies has had enough time to mature into a validated science, one that points toward a way to be "smart on crime."

The blueprint has been over forty years in the making. The challenge now is not to determine what to do, but to figure out how to get people to do it, to change their habits and long-held beliefs. How do we move people away from entrenched personal opinions? How do we counteract the sensationalized stories on the news? This might seem like stand' in front of an avalanche with a snow shovel, but if everyon volved in the work, everyone who cared about victims, e one who cared about helping young people, and everyone who cared about safer communities took up a shovel, we wouldn't feel nearly as overwhelmed.

In practical terms, we wouldn't need the number of institutions we have now. There will always be a need for detention and long-term lockup to ensure community safety, but we've come to rely on them as our best response rather than treating them as only one part of an overall approach to juvenile delinquency. We rely on them so heavily, in fact, that we have invested more resources in bricks and mortar than we have in the treatment programs these youths actually need to successfully turn their lives around. Effective delinquency reduction strategies combine corrections responses with treatment.

Effective strategies should also focus on changing the attitudes, beliefs, and values that reinforce offenders' criminal behavior. This approach teaches the offenders to (1) pay attention to their thoughts and feelings; (2) recognize how those thoughts and feelings lead to negative behavior; (3) use new thinking to reduce risk; and (4) practice, practice, and practice those new thinking and positive behavioral skills. This is not something that can be done in a classroom setting. Offenders must be given daily opportunities to practice on their own, especially since intensive repetition is a key to the intervention's success. Without it, the approach is nothing more than a lecture, and will never effectively reduce delinquency.

Effective practices to reduce delinquency are not found in any one program. They are part of a strategy, a way of thinking and acting that should be incorporated into programs and services throughout the juvenile justice system, from drug recovery treatment to detention. Bearing in mind that the most effective response to a juvenile offender is dependent on his individual needs, strategies must be age-appropriate, gender-specific, and culturally relevant.

The principles of effective practices will not cost taxpayers vast amounts of money. They are relatively easy to incorporate and they require only a small budget to train staff members and build an infrastructure that supports the overall approach. Perhaps one way to confront budgetary concerns would be to revamp a funding system that often pits various programs against one another despite the obvious fact that they are all potentially related to juvenile delinquency. Why should drug rehab programs fight for funds with child abuse prevention programs? Both are necessary. Studies have clearly shown who is most at risk in terms of juvenile delinquency, and it's necessary to address these risk areas as early in life as possible, not only for purposes of delinquency prevention, but also to protect these children. It follows that funding should be supplied to both programs, not to one over the other.

We will never be able to completely eliminate juvenile delinquency. There will always be youths who appear to be low risk but who end up committing horrible crimes, as well as high-risk juveniles who never commit any serious crimes. There will also be the anomaly: the very young offender who does not fit into any established profile, the seven-, eight-, or nine-year-old who murders or brutally attacks a classmate. Our expectations shouldn't be wildly exaggerated, but there's no reason to believe that we can't seriously address the problems.

We know which teenagers are at increased jeopardy for delinquency, and we know what works to reduce that jeopardy. The impact of services that combine corrections with treatment has been well documented by four decades of research. This balanced approach, based on solid evidence, must be utilized. Simply put, it works.

What do we do from here? Many things can help these ideas from the realm of discussion into the realm icy and practice, help move the knowledge from the l the few to the hands of everyone working in the field across the country. First, federal and local juvenile justice funds should be allocated only to programs and institutions that use the principles of effective practices. Citizens can ask their local juvenile departments if they are using their local tax dollars on these types of interventions. Political debates should include questions regarding the politicians' knowledge and support of these practices. It may seem like a daunting challenge to fully and nationally implement the effective delinquency reduction strategies, but is it any more challenging than Art overcoming his family's legacy of crime, or Rachel overcoming child abuse and institutional violence, or Tyrone overcoming his physical handicap? If they can move forward in the aftermath of such trauma, surely we, as a thoughtful nation, can find ways to bring these services to delinquent youths. We absolutely can, and in the process we can turn young people's lives around. If the large-scale changes sound too difficult to tackle, then start with the simple ones. Find out about a youth in trouble and serve as a mentor, or go to your local detention center and find out if there are kids who aren't receiving visitors on visitation day, and then ask if you can be trained as someone who just sits and listens to them. Let them know that regardless of how they feel right now, they are not alone. Plant a seed. One day, when they're ready, they will use that seed to help them move beyond their pain. Like the individuals who made a difference in the lives of the young people in this book, offer a small gesture that leads to grand action. And be aware that all of your interactions with teenagers mean something to them—that each of our words and actions matters—it all matters.

Source Material

All of the information in this book concerning what works and the history of the juvenile justice system is quoted directly or summarized from the following sources:

Andrews, D. A. (1994). "An Overview of Treatment Effectiveness: Research and Clinical Principles." Department of Psychology, Carleton University, Ottawa Canada.

Aos, Steve, Polly Phipps, Robert Barnoski, and Roxanne Lieb (1999). "The Comparative Costs and Benefits of Programs to Reduce Crime: A Review of National Research Findings with Implications for Washington State." Washington State Institute for Public Policy, Olympia, Wash.

Bishop, Donna, et al. (1996). "The Transfer of Juveniles to Criminal Court: Does It Make a Difference?" *Crime and Delinquency* 42, no. 171

Chamberlain, Patti, Ph.D., and Dr. Mark Eddy (1997). "Predict* Juvenile Recidivism." Oregon Social Learning Center prese* tion to the Lane County Public Safety Coordinating Cou*

Christy, Joe (2002). "Effective Practices—Juvenile Justice." Hand-out at "What Works" Conference, Corvallis, Ore. The conference was funded by the Community Corrections Division of the National Institute of Corrections (NIC).

Eddy, J. M., and L. Swanson-Gribskov (1998). "Juvenile Justice and Delinquency Prevention in the United States: The Influence of Theories and Traditions on Policies and Practices." In T. P. Gullota, G. R. Adams, and R. Montemayor, eds., *Delinquent Violent Youth*, Thousand Oaks, Calif.: Sage, 12–52.

Howell, James C., ed. (1995). "Guide for Implementing the Comprehensive Strategy for Serious, Violent, and Chronic Juvenile Offenders." National Council on Crime and Delinquency, Developmental Research and Programs, Inc., United States Department of Justice, June.

Kurz, Gwen (1998). Conference presentation on the paper "The 8 Percent Problem: Chronic Juvenile Offender Recidivism." Orange County, Calif. Probation Department, Program Planning and Research Division.

Latessa, Edward (1999). "Promoting Public Safety Using Effective Interventions with Offenders." Lecture given at "What Works" Conference, March 2002, Corvallis, Ore. The conference was funded by the Community Corrections Division of the National Institute of Corrections (NIC).

Office of Justice Programs (1995). "Preventing Crime: What Works, What Doesn't, What's Promising." Research report. University of Maryland, Department of Criminology and Criminal Justice.

Office of Juvenile Justice and Delinquency Prevention. Department of Justice. Juvenile Court Statistics 2003–2004. National Juvenile Court Data Archive (Pittsburgh, Pa.).

Sherman, Lawrence, et al. (1997). "Preventing Crime: What Works, What Doesn't, What's Promising." University of Maryland, Department of Criminology and Criminal Justice. Office of Justice Programs, U.S. Department of Justice.

Sprague, Jeffrey, Ph.D. (2003). "Juvenile Crime Prevention Plan Interim Report." University of Oregon, Institution on Violence and Destructive Behavior, in cooperation with Northwest Professional Consortium.

U.S. Department of Health and Human Services (2001). "Youth Violence: A Report of the Surgeon General."

U.S. Department of Justice (2000). "Promoting Public Safety Using Effective Interventions with Offenders." Sponsored by the National Institute of Corrections, the International Community Corrections Association, and state and local corrections agencies.

Wagner, Linda (2003). Juvenile Recidivism Data. Research and Development, Lane County Department of Youth Services, Eugene, Ore.